OVERVIEW

Overview

Many managers, perhaps yourself included, think that if they want a job done right, they'd better do it themselves. Maybe you've had a negative experience delegating in the past and were disappointed with the results. Or perhaps you have perfectionist tendencies, and believe you can do the job better than anyone else.

Possibly you don't delegate often because you simply don't know where to begin or how to do it effectively. Regardless of your own experience with delegating, chances are if you don't delegate, you have way too much on your plate.

When you insist on doing everything yourself, as many managers tend to do, you're not devoting your full attention to your true responsibilities as a manager – coaching, motivating, planning, and monitoring.

This course will provide you with the information and tools you need to begin delegating effectively. In it, you'll learn several key aspects of delegating:

- exactly what delegation involves and how it can benefit you, your employees, and
- the organization the qualities that all good delegators have in common, and
- the four different delegation styles.

Whether you've never delegated before or are a seasoned delegator, this course will show you how to use delegation to empower your employees to take responsibility for tasks. Instead of worrying that the job won't be done right, you'll be confident that your employees know just what to do. And even more importantly, you'll no longer waste time doing tasks that could be better done by someone else. You'll be able to get back to doing your real job – managing.

Do you remember when you first started working in business? You probably got that job because you had special abilities or skills your employer found valuable. Now think about your first good performance review or promotion. It's likely you were praised or rewarded because you were detail-oriented, took responsibility for completing tasks yourself, and didn't try to pass your work on to other people. Well, now you're a manager and it's time to let go of all that.

It's often a little shocking for people to realize that the very qualities that made them good employees may hold them back as managers. After all, it was those traits that allowed them to become managers in the first place. But management involves a special skill – delegation. Delegating involves letting go of doing everything yourself, and learning to get things done through other people.

Delegation Essentials

There are four steps in the task delegation process. First, choose which task to delegate. Then select the person to perform the task. Next, assign the task to the person. And finally, monitor the person's performance and give feedback.

In this course, you'll learn how to implement the four steps of task delegation to delegate work effectively. You'll discover how to determine which tasks should or shouldn't be delegated, and how to choose the right people for those tasks. You'll discover the best way to assign tasks so your employees understand and accept their new responsibilities. You'll also learn how to monitor your employees, and give feedback that will help them be successful at their delegated tasks.

It seems like delegating work should be simple – just ask someone to do it, and that's one less thing for you to worry about. But even when you've done your best to match the right task with the right person, problems can arise. Delegation is a learning process – for you and for your team.

Sometimes, the task you've delegated isn't finished on time. Or the result isn't what you expected. And the reason things go wrong isn't always as clear as it might seem. If an employee keeps coming to you for help with every little problem, is that because the employee's incompetent? Maybe the employee just lacks the confidence to make decisions. Or maybe your instructions for the task weren't as thorough as you thought they were.

In this course, you'll learn about some of the issues you face as a delegator. You'll learn how to avoid overcommitting your best performers and the importance of giving clear direction when you delegate a task. You'll find out when "good enough" is good enough. And you'll learn about the importance of setting up communication.

You'll also find out about employee skill problems that can slow things down. You'll learn what to do when your employees can't make decisions or turn small problems into major obstacles. And you'll find out about improving time management and technical skills.

You'll learn about some attitudes that aren't helping your employees, whether they lack motivation, take on too much work, or lack confidence. You'll have the chance to practice what you've learned by finding the root cause of delegation problems and coming up with the appropriate solution. And you'll be on track to a better understanding of how to solve the issues that arise with the tasks you delegate.

AN INTRODUCTION TO DELEGATING

An Introduction to Delegating

Learning how to delegate effectively means giving employees the authority to make decisions needed to carry out job-related tasks without constant supervision.

There are four key concepts that are directly related to delegation: empowerment, responsibility, authority, and accountability. It's also important to understand what delegation isn't – simple task assignment, dumping, or abdication.

Effective delegation is important for many reasons, and has several benefits for managers, employees, and the organization as a whole.

Understanding the principles of how to delegate effectively and how it can benefit you, your employees, and your organization will help you become a truly superior manager.

Learning to be a good delegator can make you a better manager because you'll have more time to focus on your most important job – managing. All good delegators share four key characteristics.

They have good communication skills. They also have trust in their employees, and they understand their responsibilities and know which tasks they should delegate and which they should not. Finally, good delegators are willing to take calculated risks.

To delegate effectively, you should match your delegation style with the task you're assigning. This means having an understanding of what each delegation style involves. The four different delegation styles are controlling, coaching, consulting, and coordinating.

The controlling style is used when delegating tasks to an individual who has limited experience. The coaching style should be used when delegating tasks to employees with a moderate amount of experience. The consulting style is used when delegating to employees who have had previous experience with similar tasks. Finally, when you use the coordinating style, you assign full responsibility for completing the task to the employee you're delegating to.

WHAT IS DELEGATION?

What is delegation?

After months of trying to arrange his busy schedule, Pedro, a high-level manager, is finally able to meet Julia, another manager, for lunch. The conversation turns to work and they come to the conclusion that their approaches to their jobs couldn't be more different. Pedro prefers to do everything himself, and has been feeling burned out for a long time. Julia, on the other hand, frequently assigns tasks to her employees and empowers them to make decisions. She rarely experiences work-related stress.

Question

Based on what you know about Pedro and Julia, which of the two managers do you think is more effective at delegation?

Options:
1. Julia
2. Pedro

Answer:

Option 1: This is the correct option. Delegation means giving others the authority to make decisions and carry out job-related tasks. Julia has figured out that effective delegation frees up her time and reduces her stress.

Option 2: This option is incorrect. When people don't delegate effectively, it can lead to frustration and stress. Pedro could benefit from learning how to delegate, which would free him up to focus on managing effectively.

So what exactly is delegation? It's not about simply handing unpleasant tasks to your employees. Instead, delegation means giving employees at a lower organizational level the authority to make the decisions needed to carry out job-related tasks. This doesn't mean you should assign a task and forget about it – you may need to do some coaching to ensure the employee understands what's expected. However, in delegation, the subordinate has the authority required to do the task without constant supervision.

You may be thinking that the concept of delegation seems fairly straightforward, and it is. But if you want to master the art of delegating effectively, you need to know the four key concepts that go hand in hand with delegation. These are empowerment, responsibility, authority, and accountability.

See each of the key concepts to learn more about it.

Empowerment

If you don't empower your employee, you'll still have responsibility for a task that you've delegated. Empowerment shifts the responsibility to the employee. You'll still most likely check in and monitor performance, but when you empower employees to make decisions, they use their own self-discipline to take ownership of the task.

Responsibility

When you hand over an assignment, you're giving responsibility to your employee or team – you're giving them control over the assignment. You're not telling them how to complete the assignment, but you are setting clear expectations about the results you want.

Authority

When you're delegating, authority refers to the power you give an employee or team to act and make decisions as required. You must communicate boundaries and any necessary criteria that might exist, such as budget or time considerations.

Accountability

When you delegate, you assign accountability to the employee or team. They must answer for their own actions and decisions and accept the penalties that might stem from poor judgment. On the other hand, employees enjoy the rewards that come from making good decisions.

Follow along as Julia, a manager at a commercial real estate company, delegates a task to her employee, Taku.

Julia: Hi Taku. I just found out I have to go away for a few days to attend a meeting at headquarters, and won't be able to get to some research I really need to do. I'd like you to help me.

Taku: Sure thing. What do you need me to do?

Julia: I need to find office space for a new client. I'll send you an e-mail with all the requirements. We need to find three suitable options for the client to check out by Tuesday.

Taku: I can do that. Should I call you with any questions?

Julia: No, you'll have all the information you need. I'm trusting your judgment and know you can make any decisions about issues that come up. You can call my cell phone in an emergency, but I'm giving you full responsibility for this task.

Taku: Not a problem Julia. I'll find the client the perfect space!

Julia effectively delegated a task to Taku. By giving him full responsibility for finding new office space, Julia empowered him to make decisions.

She'll be able to leave the office with the peace of mind that the task will be completed, which frees her up to focus on her meeting.

Question

Match each of the key concepts relating to delegation to the appropriate example.

Options:

A. Empowerment
B. Responsibility
C. Authority
D. Accountability

Targets:

1. You assign a task to an employee and tell him that you'll check in with him in two days to determine his progress

2. When you give an employee a task, you let her know when it's due but give her control over how she completes it

3. You give an employee the power to make decisions about a task you've assigned within a certain budgetary limit

4. When an employee doesn't complete a task on time, you tell him he has to stay late until it's finished
Answer:
Empowerment shifts the responsibility to the employee. Even though you'll still check in and monitor his performance, you're empowering the employee to make decisions.

Giving an employee responsibility means you give her control over the assignment. You don't tell her how to complete the assignment, but you do set clear expectations about the results you want.

When you're delegating, authority refers to the power you give an employee or team to act and make decisions as required. You must communicate boundaries or vital criteria, such as budget or time considerations.

Delegating means assigning accountability to the employee, who must answer for his own actions and decisions and accept the penalties that might stem from poor judgment.

Now that you know what delegation is, it's time to learn what delegation is not. Simply put, delegation isn't about simple task assignment, dumping, or abdication.

See each term to learn more about tasks that aren't considered to be delegation.

Simple task assignment

Simple task assignment means getting employees to perform duties and tasks that are part of their job descriptions. That's not delegating – that's simply expecting employees to fulfill the responsibilities of their positions.

For instance, if a sales representative's duties involve making cold calls, giving him a list of potential clients to call is simple task assignment, not delegation.

Dumping

Dumping means assigning tasks that you don't want to perform yourself. Dumping can be particularly problematic because employees can quickly grow resentful and feel that you're handing over all the unpleasant assignments to them.

For example, say you hate proofreading sales reports, but it's one of your responsibilities as a manager. Assigning this task to an employee is dumping, not delegation.

Abdication

Abdication means that you relinquish total control of the assignment. Delegation is not about abdication – you still have the ultimate accountability for the task. You should ensure that you put appropriate controls in place and monitor progress throughout the assignment without telling employees how to complete the task.

For instance, suppose you give an employee responsibility for taking care of an important customer who is unhappy. Abdication would be telling the employee to do whatever it takes to make the customer happy and leaving the office for three days without checking in. Delegation would be telling the employee to do whatever it takes to make the customer happy within a certain budget, and checking back in 24 hours to monitor progress.

Question

Determine which tasks are examples of delegation and which are not by matching the task to the appropriate

category. Each category may match to more than one task.
Options:
A. You give an accounting employee full responsibility for choosing a new payroll system and getting it set up

B. You assign a task to an employee and, when he doesn't complete it on time, require that he stays late to finish up

C. You ask your assistant to photocopy some documents for you

D. You dislike reviewing sales figures, so you pass the task over to an employee

Targets:
1. Delegation
2. Not delegation

Answer:
Giving an employee full responsibility for choosing a new payroll system and setting it up is an example of delegation. Another example of delegation is assigning a task to an employee and requiring him to stay late when he doesn't finish on time.

When you assign simple tasks that are part of an employee's job description such as photocopying, or assign tasks you don't want to do yourself such as reviewing sales figures, you aren't delegating.

BENEFITS OF DELEGATION

Benefits of delegation

Remember Pedro? He's a manager who isn't good at delegating and prefers to do things himself. As a result, he's stressed out and exhausted. If he really thought about it, Pedro could probably spot signs that he should delegate a little more. Perhaps you might recognize some of these symptoms yourself.

Are you making all the decisions or frequently missing your own deadlines? Are some employees much busier than others, while some competent employees feel frustrated and bored? Are you too busy to talk to employees or take vacations? Finally, do you regularly take work home? If you answered yes to any of these questions, you could probably benefit from learning to delegate more effectively.

Effective delegation is important for many reasons, and has a variety of benefits for managers, employees, and the organization as a whole.

Do you feel like you have too much to do and not enough time to do it in? As a manager, delegation will help you free up your time so you can focus on the important aspects of your job.

Sometimes, you can get so caught up in performing tasks unrelated to your job that you have no time to focus on your real functions, such as planning, business analysis, dealing with people problems, and controlling operations.

Another benefit of delegation is that you'll discover your employees' capabilities. Perhaps you aren't aware of how talented the people on your team really are. By delegating and assigning responsibility, you can improve trust and show employees you feel they're up to new challenges.

Question

How can effective delegating benefit you, the manager?

Options:

1. You'll have more time to focus on the important parts of your job

2. You'll find out what your employees are capable of

3. You'll improve trust as you learn that employees can do the work you assign them

4. You'll be able to hand over all the tasks you find unpleasant

5. You'll be able to abdicate responsibility for more tasks, which will free up your time for more important functions

Answer:

Option 1: This option is correct. Delegation can help you free up time so you can focus on the important aspects of your job, such as planning, business analysis, dealing with problems, and controlling operations.

Option 2: This option is correct. Delegation can help you discover your employees' capabilities and learn more about their talents and aptitudes.

Option 3: This option is correct. Delegating and assigning responsibility can improve trust and show employees you feel they're up to new challenges.

Option 4: This option is incorrect. Delegation isn't about dumping tasks you don't want to do on employees; it's about freeing up your time to focus on the important functions of your job.

Option 5: This option is incorrect. Delegating can help you free up your time so you can focus on the important parts of your job. However, you don't do it by abdicating responsibility – you still need to monitor employees' performance to ensure they stay on track.

There's no doubt that delegating can help you, but it can also benefit your employees. By assigning responsibility for a task, you provide employees with professional growth opportunities as they develop new knowledge and competencies.

Training programs are beneficial, but real assignments give employees the chance to actually use their skills.

Every assignment can be a chance for employees to learn how to accept responsibility, plan, and work collaboratively with others.

Remember how delegation benefits you by improving trust? Well, it also benefits employees by giving them a vote of confidence that you trust their abilities. Increasing self-image is a great way to improve self-esteem. And employees with positive attitudes about their abilities typically perform better, since they're more confident in their skills.

Question
How can effective delegating benefit employees?
Options:
1. They'll develop new knowledge and competencies
2. They'll have enhanced self-esteem
3. They'll be more eager to take on new training
4. They'll be happier in their jobs

Answer:
Option 1: This option is correct. Delegation provides employees with opportunities for professional growth as they develop new knowledge and competencies. For instance, delegating can teach employees how to accept responsibility, plan, and work collaboratively with others.

Option 2: This option is correct. When you delegate to employees, you're showing them that you trust their abilities. This can increase their self-esteem.

Option 3: This option is incorrect. Delegating can teach employees new skills, such as how to accept responsibility, plan, and work collaboratively with others, but it won't necessarily increase their desire for new training programs.

Option 4: This option is incorrect. Even though delegating can be a great way to improve employees' self-esteem, there's no guarantee that they'll be happier in their jobs.

It's not just managers and workers who benefit from delegation. The entire organization can reap the rewards of effective delegation as well.

Delegation can save money. When managers aren't wasting energy on tasks that can be handled by others, they can make much better use of their time. This can save the company money by not having to pay for people working inefficiently.

Organizations can also benefit from the fact that delegation promotes teamwork, and increases productivity and efficiency.

One of the most important benefits delegation can have for your organization comes through dealing with customers.

Because subordinates typically deal with customers and the daily workings of the business, empowering employees often leads to decisions that positively impact the company.

Imagine that Angus is the vice president of research and development at a large clothing manufacturer. He has recently increased the number of noncritical tasks that he delegates to his team members.

For instance, he asked his administrative assistant to take over the handling of process equipment requests from the researchers and developers.

He also sent Geoff, the chief developer, to a meeting about company sales goals that Angus didn't have time to attend himself. Geoff later relayed the important information to Angus, and felt great that Angus trusted him enough to let him attend the meeting.

Employees in Angus's department have prospered under a manager who places a high priority on effective delegation. The employees feel energized by the positive atmosphere at the facility and look forward to going to work and contributing to the company's success. The positive energy at the company is contagious. Employees are constantly striving to increase production and sales efficiency.

Delegation Essentials

Effective delegation allows you to pass on noncritical tasks. This reduces your workload, makes more time available to you, and allows you to be more productive.

Understanding how to delegate effectively will help you become a truly superior manager.

Question

In what ways can effective delegating benefit your organization?

Options:

1. It can save the company money
2. It can lead to increased productivity
3. It can promote teamwork
4. It can dramatically increase profits
5. It can help weed out the poor performers in your organization

Answer:

Option 1: This option is correct. Delegation can save money by allowing managers to make better use of their time, thus using resources more wisely.

Option 2: This option is correct. When managers delegate tasks to employees, they're able to make better use of their time, which increases productivity.

Option 3: This option is correct. Delegation often means people work closely together toward the same goal, which promotes teamwork.

Option 4: This option is incorrect. Although delegation can save the company money, a dramatic increase in profits usually involves many other factors as well.

Option 5: This option is incorrect. Delegation can help you identify your employees' capabilities, but it's not intended to single out those who don't perform as well.

WHAT MAKES A GOOD DELEGATOR?

What makes a good delegator?

If you were asked to list the qualities that make a good manager, you'd probably have no problem. But what if someone asked you to describe what makes a good delegator – would that be as easy?

As a manager, delegating effectively is a significant part of your job. Think about your own management style.

- Do you delegate effectively? To find out, think about what your answers would be to several questions:
- Do you tell all your employees what's expected of them?
- Do you regularly involve employees in activities related to problem solving, goal setting, and productivity improvement?
- Do you emphasize motivating, controlling, and planning over doing tasks that could be done by others?
- Do you carefully match the employee to the task?

- If you've assigned a task and issues occur, do you give the employee a chance to solve any problems before stepping in?
- When you delegate, do you give the employee full details about the task?
- Do you perceive delegation as a way to help employees develop knowledge, skills, and expertise?

Question

Now think about the list of questions you just considered.

Based on your answers, how do you think you rate as a delegator?

Options:

1. Excellent
2. Average
3. Poor

Answer:

Option 1: It's great that you rated yourself as an excellent delegator. You probably have good communication skills and trust in your employees. You most likely understand your own responsibilities and are probably willing to take risks. These are all qualities of a good delegator. In this topic, you'll learn how to hone your skills and become an even better delegator.

Option 2: You rated yourself as an average delegator. That means you probably possess some of the qualities that make a great delegator, but feel like you could use some work on others. This topic will give you the tools you need so that you can think of yourself as an excellent delegator instead of an average one.

Option 3: You rated yourself as a poor delegator. This could be because you have a fear of losing control, or perhaps you lack confidence in your employees. Whatever the reason, taking this topic will greatly improve your skills as a delegator. After taking it, you may even rate yourself as excellent.

Perhaps you'd like to be a better delegator, but aren't sure where to begin. Quite often, managers make excuses – either to themselves or to others – about why they don't delegate. However, in almost every case, there are actions you can take to overcome the excuse. How many of these excuses have you heard or even used yourself?

See each excuse to find out the actions that can be taken to overcome it.

"I have no confidence in my employees"

If you don't have confidence in your employees, you can start by delegating small tasks to build confidence gradually.

"I like things done my way"

It's OK to prefer things be done to your specifications, but instead of doing it all yourself, simply communicate your preferences and standards.

"My staff will resent the extra work"

It's true that employees may resent extra work. However, the best employees will appreciate you giving them opportunities to grow professionally.

"I can't trust anyone to do it right"

You don't want to hand over tasks for which employees have no training or experience. But, if you've given them the right training and experience, there are countless tasks you can delegate with confidence.

"I can do it better myself"

You may indeed be able to do most tasks better yourself, but that doesn't mean you should. Many tasks are more suited to employees with a lower level of responsibility, and you shouldn't hesitate to delegate to them.

"It's quicker and easier to do it myself"

Delegation does require that you spend time and energy explaining tasks up front, which is why it seems faster and easier to just do the task yourself. But time you spend on tasks that could be done by others is time taken from higher-value activities that your employees aren't capable of doing.

"I'm a doer, not a delegator"

Before you became a manager, you were probably great at doing certain tasks and may have received recognition for your contributions. As a manager, it can be hard to let go and focus on your new responsibilities – leading, motivating, and planning. But now that you're a manager, it's time to let others do the doing while you do the managing.

"I'm responsible for what happens around here"

Some managers fear losing control and feel that delegating means giving away part of their authority. That's simply not the case – delegating does not mean abdicating responsibility.

It should be pretty clear by now why so many managers have trouble delegating. But what exactly makes someone a good delegator? Consider Norman. He's the manager of operations at a large furniture wholesaler. His employees all like him, and more importantly, feel he delegates fairly and effectively.

They might have a hard time pinpointing exactly why, but Norman's employees would all agree that Norman possesses the four attributes shared by all good delegators: he has good communication skills, he trusts his employees, he understands his responsibilities, and he's willing to take risks.

GOOD COMMUNICATION SKILLS

Good communication skills

The first attribute shared by effective delegators is good communication skills. This means they can explain expectations and desired outcomes clearly. They remember the details employees will need to know and use good questioning techniques to check for understanding. They ask if employees have questions and listen to their responses. Finally, they're able to encourage employees and express confidence with sincerity.

See each aspect of being a good communicator, in order, to learn more about it.

Explain expectations and desired outcomes

The ability to explain your expectations and desired outcomes clearly is one of the best indicators of a successful delegator. Employees can't read your mind, so you must clearly articulate what you want.

Recently, Norman asked Vonzell to source a fabric supplier. Instead of giving the vague direction to find a new supplier, he stated, "Please find a company within

100 miles that offers same-day shipping." Vonzell didn't have to guess what Norman wanted – he was very clear.

Remembering the details

Part of being a good communicator is remembering the details employees will need to know. If you forget to provide all the relevant information, employees will have to come back to you with more questions.

Norman remembers to provide Vonzell with contact information for all the possible suppliers she should contact so she won't waste time searching.

Using good questioning techniques

Being a good communicator means not waiting until you're finished explaining a task to ensure the employee knows what's expected. Using good questioning techniques to check for understanding as you go means you won't have to explain things twice or backtrack.

After he explains to Vonzell that she is to find a new fabric supplier, Norman asks, "Do you understand what I want you to do?" He then goes on to explain that the task needs to be completed by Friday. Before he leaves her to the assignment, Norman asks Vonzell if she has any questions or concerns.

Asking if employees have questions

It's likely that employees will have questions when you've finished explaining a task. If they aren't asking questions on their own, be sure to initiate a dialog by asking if they have any concerns. When employees do respond with questions, listen with empathy.

When Norman asks Vonzell if she has any questions or concerns, she responds that Friday might not be a manageable deadline. Norman responds, "I understand it seems like a lot of work for such a short time frame. I think once you start working on this though, you'll find opportunities to save time." By empathizing with her concerns, Norman shows Vonzell that he was listening.

Be encouraging and express confidence

Good communicators are able to be encouraging and express confidence with sincerity. Employees can usually tell when you're not being sincere, so be honest in your encouragement.

When Vonzell told Norman she wasn't sure she'd be able to meet the deadline he set, Norman said, "Vonzell, I've seen you meet shorter deadlines than this in the past. I know you're capable, and you'll do great!"

Question

What are examples of appropriate questions or statements a delegating manager might say?

Options:

1. "I need you to reorganize the filing system so companies with numbers in their names are at the beginning."

2. "I've created a document with all the information you'll need to complete the task."

3. "So that's pretty much what I need. Do you have any questions before we continue?"

4. "Do you have any concerns about your ability to complete the assignment?"

5. "I know you've never done anything like this before, but you're a hard worker and I know you can do it."

6. "If you can't do the assignment, I'll just get someone else to do it."

Answer:

Option 1: This option is correct. Good communicators have the ability to explain their expectations and desired outcomes clearly.

Option 2: This option is correct. Being a good communicator means remembering to provide employees with all the details they'll need to know.

Option 3: This option is correct. Don't wait until you're finished explaining a task to ensure the employee knows what's expected. Use good questioning techniques to check for understanding as you go so you won't have to explain things twice or backtrack.

Option 4: This option is correct. If employees don't ask questions on their own, you should initiate dialog by asking if they have any questions or concerns. When employees do respond with questions, listen with empathy.

Option 5: This option is correct. Being a good communicator means having the ability to be encouraging and express confidence with sincerity. Employees can usually tell when you're not being sincere, so be honest in your encouragement.

Option 6: This option is incorrect. To be a good communicator, you should be encouraging and express confidence with sincerity. If an employee doesn't feel up to the task, try to find out why – chances are, she just doesn't have enough information to feel confident.

TRUST IN EMPLOYEES

Trust in employees

The second attribute that good delegators have in common is trust in their employees to perform tasks that they, as managers, are ultimately responsible for.

If you want to be perceived as a trusting delegator, you should support employees even when their actions are criticized by others. You should back up their decisions. You shouldn't dwell on their mistakes, and you definitely shouldn't spy on them.

You should be open and forthcoming with information. Don't manipulate employees; show respect by listening to them.

You might think to yourself, "Of course I trust my employees!" But do you really? There are several actions that many managers take, whether consciously or not, that signify a lack of trust.

Have you ever taken back an assignment if the employee shows signs of trouble or confusion? This is called reverse delegation and is a sure sign that you don't fully trust the employee.

Do you keep watch over an employee's shoulder while that employee is trying to carry out a task? Do you communicate somehow – either verbally or nonverbally – that you don't have much confidence in an employee's ability to get it right? These are both actions that signify a lack of trust.

Follow along as Norman delegates a task to Mario, one of his warehouse supervisors.

Norman: Mario, I have a job I really need your help with. We need a new inventory program, and I want you to find a programmer to create one.

Mario: Wow, that sounds like a pretty big job.

Mario is worried.

Norman: You're right, it will probably be a fairly big job. But I'm asking you to handle it because you have the experience to do it right.

Mario is uncertain.

Mario: Well, thanks for the vote of confidence! I hope I can meet your expectations.

Norman: I trust you, Mario, and will be here to support you if you run into any problems, but I'm leaving the project in your hands.

Mario: Sounds great – I'll do my best!

Mario is smiling.

By assigning such an important task to Mario, Norman demonstrated trust. He was honest about the fact that it would probably be a difficult job, but expressed his confidence and offered his support without taking back the assignment, which would have been a sure sign of a lack of trust.

Question

Which statements reflect things managers who trust their employees might say?

Options:

1. "It's all right that you made a mistake. Let's just move on and get back on track."

2. "Don't worry about what the other team members say; do the task the way you think is best."

3. "Just let me know if there's any other information you need to complete the task."

4. "I'll be checking up on your progress regularly, so stay on track as best you can."

5. "If you can't finish the task, I'll just do it myself."

Answer:

Option 1: This option is correct. Trusting delegators don't dwell on employees' mistakes.

Option 2: This option is correct. Trusting delegators back up employees' decisions and support them even when their actions are criticized by others.

Option 3: This option is correct. Trusting delegators are open and forthcoming with information.

Option 4: This option is incorrect. Trusting delegators don't keep watch over an employee's shoulder while the employee is trying to carry out a task.

Option 5: This option is incorrect. Trusting delegators don't just take back an assignment if the employee shows signs of trouble or confusion.

UNDERSTAND RESPONSIBILITIES

Understand responsibilities

The third attribute good delegators possess is that they understand their own responsibilities as leaders and can identify tasks that should be delegated to others.

So which tasks should you delegate? Anything that involves day-to-day minor decisions can easily be assigned to someone else. So can minor staffing problems, such as shift changes or scheduling. You can definitely delegate tasks your employees are expected to do in your absence. Clerical duties should be delegated, as should answering routine questions – give employees a chance to think for themselves. Finally, any task that can offer employees the chance for professional development can be delegated.

If you delegate all those tasks, what's left for you to do? There are certain tasks you should never delegate, such as dealing with morale problems. Obviously you shouldn't hand over a task that no one else is qualified to do. Personnel issues, such as hiring and firing, are your responsibility, as are assignments from your boss that you're expected to do yourself. And finally, if an emergency arises and there's no time to explain a task, you shouldn't delegate – just do it yourself.

Question

Classify tasks as those that should be delegated and those that shouldn't by matching the tasks to the descriptions. Each description may have more than one match.

Options:

A. Changing the schedule so two employees can switch shifts

B. Ordering toner for the photocopier

C. Hiring a new front-desk employee

D. Dealing with an employee who is constantly complaining

Targets:

1. Should be delegated
2. Shouldn't be delegated

Answer:

Anything that involves day-to-day minor decisions, such as ordering office supplies, can easily be delegated to someone else. So can minor staffing problems, such as shift changes or scheduling.

You should never delegate tasks involving morale problems, such as an unhappy employee, nor should you delegate personnel issues, such as hiring and firing.

WILLING TO TAKE RISKS

Willing to take risks

The final attribute shared by good delegators is that they're willing to take risks. In this case, taking risks isn't referring to thrill-seeking hobbies like bungee jumping – it means placing someone else in the position of performing tasks for which the manager is responsible.

As a manager, you take risks every time you delegate. Will employees succeed, or will they fail? You can never know for sure, but you can improve the chance of success by taking calculated risks.

When you're delegating, calculated risks helps you minimize failure by allowing you to properly evaluate the situation and communicate effectively.

For instance, investing the time and money to train an employee to take over the maintenance of a customer database is a calculated risk. You're taking a chance to find out if the employee has the skills and ability to take over the task, but minimizing the risk by providing adequate training.

Delegation Essentials

It would be great if everyone only took calculated risks, but that's not always the reality. Managers sometimes take careless risks when delegating. For instance, assigning a critical task to an unqualified or inexperienced employee is almost guaranteed to end in failure. So, too, is telling an employee to complete a job with no instruction.

Being willing to take risks in delegating can be a great way to find out which team members have the talent and skills to make it in your company, but be sure that you take calculated – not careless – risks.

Question

Classify examples as calculated risks or careless delegation by matching examples to descriptions. Each description may have more than one match.

Options:

A. Asking a new employee to immediately take over maintenance of a machine that requires months of training

B. Telling a team member to write updated instructions for a process she isn't part of

C. Having an employee take over the accounting duties you normally perform, with the company's accountant monitoring the employee for a few months

D. Tasking an employee with taking over the weekly sales meeting to find out if she has what it takes to be promoted

Targets:

1. Careless delegation
2. Calculated risk

Answer:

Asking an inexperienced employee to take on a task he's incapable of performing or assigning a task with no instruction are both examples of careless delegation.

Monitoring an employee who's learning to do a new task or giving an employee responsibility to assess her skills are both examples of calculated risks. When you're delegating, taking calculated risks helps you minimize failure by allowing you to properly evaluate the situation and communicate effectively.

DELEGATION STYLES

Delegation styles

As a manager, you're probably familiar with your own leadership style. Maybe you like to make all the decisions, or perhaps you prefer a more democratic style. But what would you say if someone asked you to describe your delegation style? Chances are you've never even given it much thought before.

Randomly assigning tasks is never a good way to delegate effectively. Effective delegation involves matching your delegation style with the task you're assigning.

Think of it this way: if you were to ask an employee to type a report, you would use a different delegation style than if you asked the same employee to research and write the report.

In order to delegate effectively, you need to understand what each delegating style involves.

Managers need to adopt different delegation styles for different employees and situations. You may even need to use all four styles in the same day, depending on the circumstances. The four different delegation styles are controlling, coaching, consulting, and coordinating.

CONTROLLING

Controlling

The controlling style is most often used when delegating tasks to an individual who has limited experience with those tasks. This style requires a substantial amount of time and input from the manager since you have to thoroughly describe the task to the employee from start to finish. This style typically results in limited responsibility for the inexperienced employee, but also less stress.

See each result of using the controlling style to learn more about how Julia, a manager, uses this style.

Limited responsibility

"I use the controlling style with inexperienced employees. When I delegate tasks using this style, I give limited responsibility to the employee performing the assignment."

Less stress

"Delegating using the controlling style can lead to decreased stress levels for inexperienced employees who require lots of guidance. I find it's a good way to ease new employees into the job and give them a chance to learn in a stress-free environment."

Say you're a manager at a software company, and you have a new administrative assistant, Wendell. You need Wendell to set up a group distribution list for an e-mail you want him to send on your behalf. It's vital that the e-mail be worded and sent properly because it's being directed at some important clients.

Wendell has never created a group distribution list before and will need some guidance.

You know that a misdirected e-mail could cause your company to lose clients, so you decide the controlling delegation style is best. You guide Wendell through the entire process of constructing and sending the e-mail. You know the message has been sent correctly.

Wendell could easily have been frustrated when he wasn't sure how to complete the task. But, with your guidance, he's now confident that he'll know how to perform similar tasks independently in the future.

As Wendell's manager, you feel confident that the controlling style was the best choice in this situation.

Question

What are the possible results of using the controlling delegating style?

Options:

1. Employees will have limited responsibility

2. New and inexperienced employees will have decreased stress levels

3. Employees will be effectively taught how to do new tasks

4. Employees will take more of the manager's time

5. Employees will have too much unstructured work time

Answer:

Option 1: This option is correct. When you use the controlling style, you'll spend more time with the employee providing guidance on how to successfully accomplish the task, which limits the employee's responsibility.

Option 2: This option is correct. When you use the controlling style, the employee completing the task isn't given a high degree of responsibility. This reduces the amount of stress associated with completing the task.

Option 3: This option is correct. When you guide an employee through the process using the controlling style, you provide a learning experience for the employee.

Option 4: This option is correct. The controlling delegating style means you control more of what is happening, which takes more time on your part.

Option 5: This option is incorrect. When you use the controlling style, the employee's work time will actually be very structured because you'll be going through each of the steps involved with performing the task.

COACHING

Coaching
The second type of delegating style is coaching. When you adopt the coaching style, you closely supervise the completion of the task, but less so than when you use the controlling style. Coaching should be used when delegating tasks to employees with a moderate amount of experience.

When you delegate using the coaching style, employees completing tasks under your supervision feel more responsibility than they do under a controlling delegator.

Because of the increased responsibility, employees tend to feel more motivated.

Imagine again that you're a manager at a software company. You're deciding whom you should ask to compile a report on consumer privacy issues and Internet usage. You definitely don't have the time to monitor every little step of the task, but you do have time to provide some coaching. The employee you select should have a moderate amount of experience, although the employee will still be well-monitored.

Delegation Essentials

You decide to delegate the task to Kirk, a software developer who has been with the company for one year. Kirk has a moderate amount of experience compiling reports.

Kirk feels some responsibility for completing the task properly. By using the coaching style, you can monitor Kirk's progress fairly closely to ensure he is doing the task correctly.

Question

When would it be best to use the coaching delegation style?

Options:

1. When the employee has a moderate amount of experience
2. When the employee is ready for more responsibility
3. When you don't want to have to supervise the employee
4. When the employee has little to no experience

Answer:

Option 1: This option is correct. You should use the coaching delegation style when you're delegating tasks to employees with a moderate amount of experience. If the employee has no experience with the particular task, it's best to use the controlling style.

Option 2: This option is correct. When you delegate using the coaching delegation style, an employee completing a task under your supervision feels more responsibility than with the controlling style.

Option 3: This option is incorrect. When you're using the coaching delegation style, you do need to closely supervise the completion of the task, but less so than when you use the controlling style.

Option 4: This option is incorrect. Actually, you use the controlling delegation style, not the coaching style, when the employee has little to no experience.

CONSULTING

Consulting

Consulting is the third delegation style. When managers use this style, they give the employee completing the task more freedom than if the controlling or coaching styles had been used. It's most appropriate to use the consulting style when you're delegating to an employee who has had previous experience with similar tasks.

The employee is responsible for completing the task independently when you use the consulting approach.

But, should the employee require support, input, or other types of assistance, the consulting manager is available as a resource.

In your role as manager of a software company, you have to delegate the task of researching and compiling a document on high-speed Internet usage by individuals in an urban setting. You would like to delegate the task to an employee who can work fairly independently. You require an experienced and reliable employee who has proven competence in the areas of researching and compiling documents.

You determine that Penny, who has been working for the company for three years, would be an ideal candidate to perform the task. You also conclude that the best style to use is the consulting style. Penny is an experienced software developer who has proven her effectiveness at researching and writing reports in the past. Penny is responsible for completing this task independently but, if she has any questions, you'll be available to give input and assist her.

Question

In which situations would it be best to adopt the consulting delegation style?

Options:

1. When delegating to an experienced employee
2. When delegating to an inexperienced employee
3. When you have a tight deadline to meet
4. When you don't have time to monitor every step of the task
5. When you wish to complete the task yourself

Answer:

Actually, it is best to use a consulting type of style when delegating tasks to experienced employees, but when you do not have time to monitor every step of the task.

Option 1: This option is correct. You should use the consulting delegation style when delegating to an experienced employee. The employee is responsible for completing the task independently, but you're there as a resource if assistance is required.

Option 2: This option is incorrect. Managers should use the controlling style, not the consulting style, when delegating to an inexperienced employee.

Option 3: This option is incorrect. When you have a tight deadline to meet, it might be more appropriate to complete the task yourself.

Option 4: This option is correct. When you use the consulting delegation style, you give the employee completing the task more freedom than if you had used the controlling or coaching styles.

Option 5: This option is incorrect. The consulting delegation style is used when you want the employee to take care of almost all aspects of the task.

COORDINATING

Coordinating

Coordinating is the fourth delegation style. When you use this style, you assign full responsibility for completing the task to the employee you're delegating to. The two key components of this style are minimal feedback and a high level of autonomy.

See each attribute to learn more about the coordinating delegation style.

Minimal feedback

When managers delegate with the coordinating style, employees don't usually seek a lot of feedback. The coordinating style should be used with experienced employees.

For instance, suppose you need to delegate the task of setting up a new database to track inventory. You assign the task to Julio, who worked as a database administrator for ten years. He doesn't require supervision and knows how to build the database without your input.

High level of autonomy

The coordinating delegation style provides employees with the most autonomy and responsibility. The result is a highly motivated and industrious workforce.

Because you're not watching over his shoulder, Julio, the employee you delegated to, isn't distracted and gets the database up and running in a few weeks. It's exactly what you wanted, and you know the coordinating delegation style was just the right one to use with Julio.

Consider this example of a manager using the different delegation styles. Michael is a departmental supervisor for a large Internet sportswear distributor. He recently hired a new administrative assistant, Ben, who just graduated from business college. One of Ben's responsibilities will be to organize Michael's customer contact list. The contacts will need to be deleted, saved in e-mail folders, or saved as hard copies. Ben has never completed this task before and Michael wants it done in a specific way.

See each delegating style to find out when Michael should use it.

Controlling

Michael will use the controlling delegation style while Ben organizes the contact list for the first couple of times. He will take the time to guide Ben through the process step by step to ensure the contact lists are placed in the proper folders, and that hard copies are made when necessary.

Coaching

After the first few times that Ben organizes the contact lists, Michael will switch to using a coaching delegation style. He will still closely monitor the way his contact lists are organized, but will give Ben a little more control over the process.

Consulting

Eventually, Michael will use the consulting delegation style with Ben for this task. After a few weeks, Ben should have enough experience to deal with organizing Michael's contact lists without a lot of monitoring or feedback being required.

Coordinating

Since Michael will deal with his customer contact lists daily and will have regular contact with Ben, the coordinating delegation style will probably not be used for contact list organization. However, that's not to say that Michael will never be able to use the coordinating style with Ben – he may use it for future tasks.

Question

When would it be best to use the coordinating delegation style?

Options:

1. When you're delegating to a very experienced employee
2. When you want to assign full responsibility for the task's completion to the employee
3. When the employee has a moderate amount of experience
4. When you have new and inexperienced employees who need to learn the ropes

Answer:

Option 1: This option is correct. The coordinating style should be used with experienced employees. As a result, they require minimal feedback.

Option 2: This option is correct. The coordinating delegation style provides employees with the most autonomy and responsibility.

Delegation Essentials

Option 3: This option is incorrect. You should use the coaching delegation style, not the coordinating style, when you're delegating tasks to employees with a moderate amount of experience.

Option 4: This option is incorrect. Actually, you should use the controlling style, not the coordinating style, with new or inexperienced employees.

It should be clear by now which delegation styles are best to use in different situations. By being able to determine the optimum delegation style, you will become a much more efficient delegator.

Question

Match the appropriate delegation style to the description of the employee to whom the task is being delegated.

Options:

A. Coordinating
B. Controlling
C. Consulting
D. Coaching

Targets:

1. Kit has been with the firm for three days and never completed such a task before
2. Pam has been with the company for nine years and has worked on several similar projects
3. Bob has worked for the agency 25 years and worked on such projects many times
4. Tate has worked with the company for one year and has done such tasks a few times

Answer:

The ability to properly match the employee experience levels with the most appropriate delegating styles will help you choose the most appropriate delegating styles to adopt in your own work environment.

This is an example of when to use the controlling delegation style. Because Kit has no experience with the task and will require a substantial amount of time and input from the manager, he'll require constant supervision.

This is an example of when to use the consulting delegation style because Pam has had previous experience with similar tasks and will be responsible for completing the task independently.

This is an example of when to use the coordinating delegation style because Bob is an experienced employee, and the manager can assign him the responsibility for completing the task.

This is an example of when to use the coaching delegation style. Tate has a moderate amount of experience and will require close supervision, but less so than if the manager were to use the controlling delegation style.

THE DELEGATION PROCESS

The Delegation Process

Delegation is the act of entrusting other people with completing tasks for which you remain responsible. Good delegation involves choosing the most efficient and effective way to budget your time and expertise.

There are three main steps in choosing tasks to delegate. First, you determine the skills you share with your employees. Next, you assess which tasks you're currently doing that fall within that shared skill set. Finally, you choose which tasks you could reasonably delegate to someone else.

Step one of task delegation is selecting the person to perform the task you're delegating. Selecting the right person involves assessing candidates' ability, availability, and reliability, as well as potential, interest, and enthusiasm.

Step two of task delegation is to assign the chosen task to the person you've selected. First, describe the task; second, motivate the employee; third, get the employee's verbal acceptance of the task.

Communication style is important. Use a positive tone and clearly describe the task. Use questions to check for understanding as you explain the task, and to gain acceptance of the task.

Step three of task delegation is monitoring performance. This step involves the post-assignment activities of managing the progress of the delegated task, and giving feedback on performance to the employee implementing that task. The best way to ensure successful delegation is to maintain an adequate level of control over the task, while avoiding micromanaging and taking back work.

Feedback is also a component of good management practice. Good feedback is descriptive, specific, timely, open, and practical.

DELEGATING APPROPRIATELY

Delegating appropriately

Delegation is entrusting other people with tasks for which you remain responsible. Effective delegation makes your job as a manager easier, and frees up time to concentrate on essential managerial tasks such as goal-setting and strategic planning. Delegation helps you develop trust and rapport with your staff. It also helps with succession planning – choosing competent employees to fill key organizational positions.

The four-step task delegation process can help you reap the benefits of task delegation efficiently and effectively. Step one of task delegation is choosing the task or tasks to delegate. To delegate, you must first assess your own responsibilities. This will allow you to determine which tasks could and should be considered for delegation. You'll need to decide what to delegate as well as what not to delegate.

So delegation begins with analysis – reviewing your work and identifying tasks that can be considered for delegation.

As a manager, your job isn't to do the work for your team members. Nor is it to pass on all your work to them. Your job is to provide the motivation, direction, information, and tools your team needs to achieve work-related goals and objectives.

For example, sales managers often delegate most of the direct selling to salespeople, while continuing to motivate their teams, and plan, monitor, and review the sales effort.

Tasks suitable for delegation are those that are routine, noncritical, and within the ability of your employees. Other suitable tasks are those that are easy to learn or that provide opportunities for development, as well as those that aren't time sensitive.

See each type of task suitable for delegation.

Routine

Routine tasks are tasks implemented on a regular basis in accordance with an established procedure. You can often delegate routine tasks such as doing paperwork, checking inventory, monitoring equipment, or taking minutes at meetings.

Noncritical

Noncritical tasks don't involve significant risk if they are not accomplished immediately or perfectly. Researching potential clients, culling files, or archiving data can be important. However, these tasks aren't likely to affect the critical path of a project or initiative.

Within the ability of employees

You may have tasks that you like doing, or that you do well, but are within the ability of employees to do as well. If someone on your team has the talent or training to accomplish a task, it can be delegated. For example, if someone has graphic skills, you could let that person design a newsletter or annual report.

Easy to learn

Do you have tasks that no one else knows how to do, but would be relatively easy to learn? If so, consider training someone else to do them. For example, tasks with clear parameters and guidelines can often be delegated with minimal explanation and instruction.

Provide opportunities

Delegating tasks can provide development opportunities for your staff. This will prepare employees for moving into positions the company needs, or will need, to fill. For example, you can encourage employees to develop new skills by asking them to attend conferences or networking events in your place.

Aren't time sensitive

Tasks that aren't time sensitive can often be delegated to employees. This gives employees time to learn how to complete the task, and to start over if they make a mistake. For example, archiving files is rarely a time-sensitive task.

Not every management task is suitable for delegation. It's important that you retain responsibility for tasks that require skills or authority only you possess. Don't delegate tasks involving leadership and strategic planning, employee matters, confidential or sensitive issues, or tasks specifically delegated to you.

See each type of task for information on what not to delegate.

Strategic planning

Strategic planning is a leadership role. Managers are responsible for establishing strategy, overseeing long-term goals and objectives, and making sure the efforts of their work units support the corporate vision.

Employee matters

Employee matters – such as hiring, firing, or taking disciplinary action – should rarely be delegated. It's important for managers to take personal responsibility for giving employees performance reviews and feedback.

Confidential or sensitive issues

Maintaining the secrecy of confidential information is a vital responsibility for a manager. It's rarely responsible or prudent to delegate tasks involving sensitive reports, legal proceedings, trade secrets, financial data, or employee information.

Tasks specifically delegated to you

Some work tasks will be assigned to you because of your specific knowledge, skills, or experience. Examples might include complex customer negotiations, meeting with important clients, or approval of expenditures.

Tasks specifically delegated to you shouldn't be redelegated to someone else. Ignoring the preferences of your superiors or important clients may raise questions about your competency and trustworthiness.

Question

Karen is a senior research manager for a cosmetics company. Match Karen's management tasks to the appropriate delegation approach. Each approach may have more than one match.

Options:

A. Writing monthly progress reports for the department
B. Drafting a long-term action plan for the department
C. Hiring a laboratory assistant
D. Attending an industry awards dinner

E. Applying for a new patent
Targets:
1. Delegate
2. Don't delegate
Answer:
Tasks suitable for delegation are those that involve routine work, work that can be performed by qualified employees, and work that provides employees with opportunities for development. These include writing progress reports and attending events.

Tasks not suitable for delegation involve hiring or firing employees, strategic planning, and dealing with confidential information. These include drafting a long-term action plan, hiring an assistant, and applying for a patent.

DETERMINING TASKS FOR DELEGATION

Determining tasks for delegation

Once you've accepted that you should be delegating tasks, the challenge becomes determining which tasks to delegate. Making those decisions is a matter of prioritization. Prioritizing means choosing the most efficient and effective way to budget your time and expertise on achieving goals and objectives.

There are three main steps in choosing tasks to delegate:

1. First of all, you should determine shared skills. These are the skills that you have in common with one or more of your employees.

2. Next, you assess your current tasks to determine if any fall within that shared skill set.

3. Finally, you choose which tasks are suitable for delegation to someone else by matching current tasks to shared skills.

Step one of choosing tasks to delegate is to determine shared skills. As a general rule, you should prioritize delegating those tasks your employees are capable of doing or can be trained to handle.

As a manager, you'll need to be familiar with the skills, capabilities, and knowledge of each of your employees – collectively known as the "talent pool." This will allow you to select someone whose potential matches the skill set needed for the task. For example, employees may have the skills to do research, compile reports, schedule meetings, check the accuracy of financial data, or provide coaching and orientation to new employees.

Step two of task delegation is to assess your current tasks. Now that you're aware of the shared skills in your work unit, it's time to assess which of the tasks you're currently handling fall within that shared skill set.

It's important to assess an entire task. Holding back steps for yourself or dividing up a task between individual employees can create confusion about authority and responsibility.

If a task is too complicated for one person, consider whether the task could be delegated to a project team. For example, a team of employees could take on responsibility for organizing a conference or annual general meeting.

Step three of task delegation is to choose tasks suitable for delegation. It may help to make a general list of your tasks and consider which tasks don't require your unique capabilities to complete.

In general, tasks involving your personal judgment aren't good candidates for delegation. Examples include hiring new team members, liaising with your superiors, or setting long-term strategic goals.

Good tasks for delegation are tasks other people could do. These might include organizing staff meetings, checking sales figures, compiling data, or doing research.

A checklist can help you choose tasks for delegation. A delegation checklist has three simple steps.

For step one, you would make a list of tasks. For example: organize weekly staff meetings, check monthly sales figures, hire new staff members, approve budget changes, compile customer data, research target markets, and liaise with board of directors.

Step two is to determine tasks that are suitable for delegation, and step three is to place a check mark next to suitable tasks.

You're a senior manager at a large investment firm. Your department has a number of support staff and three direct reports. Rosa is the assistant manager. She's been with the company for ten years and has excellent organization and communication skills. Tyrell is a former graphic designer who has worked for you for three years. And Mario is your newest employee. He has recently finished college and just started working for you.

Question

Based on the skills you share with Rosa, Tyrell, and Mario, which of the tasks on your list are appropriate to delegate?

Options:

1. Choose a font and layout for the department's annual general report

2. Assess the department's progress toward achieving strategic objectives

3. Prepare a confidential report for the company's chief financial officer

4. Teach new employees how to use the company's telephone system

5. Conduct annual performance reviews of employees

6. Book a conference room for monthly staff meetings

Answer:

Option 1: This option is correct. This task could be delegated to Tyrell because of his graphic design skills.

Option 2: This option is incorrect. Leadership functions such as planning strategy are generally not suitable for delegation.

Option 3: This option is incorrect. Even though you trust your employees, confidential matters are best handled by the manager to whom they're assigned.

Option 4: This option is correct. This task could be delegated to Rosa. She has good communication skills and is an experienced employee.

Option 5: This option is incorrect. Performance reviews require personal judgment and assessment. These types of tasks are rarely suitable for delegation.

Option 6: This option is correct. Routine tasks that are easily learned are good tasks for delegation. Any of your employees could learn to complete this task.

DELEGATION CRITERIA

Delegation criteria

Not everyone can do the same work to the same degree of effectiveness. People within a business organization possess a variety of skills, talents, and personalities. In fact, it's this diversity that allows people to do their jobs, and enables the organization to function efficiently.

Step two of task delegation is selecting the person to perform the task you're delegating. Delegating tasks is beneficial to both you and your staff. Delegation helps improve the capabilities of employees and gives you time for managerial and strategic work. Taking their skills and available time into account, you could consider delegating many technical, routine, or noncritical tasks to employees.

In step one of task delegation, you determine the types of tasks that can be delegated. But it's not enough just to make a subjective match between the requirements of the task and the perceived skills in your talent pool. There are other characteristics that are vital to delegating the right task to the right person. Selecting the right people involves assessing not only their ability, but their availability and reliability.

See each characteristic for more information on selecting the right person for the task.

Ability

One of the most important characteristics to consider when selecting the right person for the task is the person's ability to do the job. This may seem obvious, but there are a number of factors to consider. Technical knowledge, skills, and track record are good indicators of ability. However, you also have to consider the personality, attitude, and authority level of the employee.

Availability

Even if your employee is capable of doing the task, it's important to make sure that person has the time available to handle the delegated task. Availability problems result when work is assigned to employees who are already fully occupied with their own jobs. Check with the employee to make sure your request is reasonable and can be carried out in the time allotted.

If an employee doesn't have enough time, there's a risk the delegated task won't be completed or will be executed poorly. It's also possible that the employee's regular job performance will suffer.

Reliability

When you delegate tasks to employees, you need to be able to trust them to get the job done. Reliability consists of behavioral consistency and integrity.

Employees differ in their response to delegated responsibilities. Some consistently underestimate their ability to handle something new. Others may prioritize regular tasks over the delegated task, or they may have poor time-management skills. Past performance is a good indicator of the reliability of an employee. Look for someone with a good track record of dealing with delegation.

Question

What are the most important characteristics to consider when delegating tasks to employees?

Options:

1. You can rely on the employee
2. The employee has the ability to do the task
3. The employee is available to do the task
4. You have the authority to compel them to do the task 5. The task is easy to do

Answer:

Option 1: This option is correct. Reliability means you can trust employees to get the job done.

Option 2: This option is correct. Ability means employees are capable of doing the task.

Option 3: This option is correct. Availability means employees have time to do the task well.

Option 4: This option is incorrect. As a manager, you need the authority to assign tasks, but it won't do you any good if employees don't have the ability or availability to do the task.

Option 5: This option is incorrect. Simple tasks are suitable for delegation. However, delegating an employee capable of doing the task is more important than the degree of difficulty.

When you delegate, it's critical to understand ability, availability, and reliability. But there are other characteristics that are also important. An employee's potential, interest, and enthusiasm are additional factors that you should consider when you delegate.

See each characteristic for more information on how it influences delegation.

Potential

When you assign a task, you not only have to consider who can do the task, but who also has the potential to learn the task. Training enables employees to handle new tasks, and it also makes them more comfortable and confident with taking on greater responsibilities.

Interest

Delegation can provide good opportunities for employees to gain skills and develop their careers. Think about which employees have expressed interest in growth and development, and which tasks would be suitable to delegate to them.

Enthusiasm

Enthusiasm is a good indicator of an employee's initiative. Enthusiastic employees have the motivation and willingness to accept new challenges. You won't get the best work from an employee who isn't willing to take on new tasks.

There are many considerations when deciding who to select for a particular task. For example, what do you do if an employee has some essential characteristics, but not all of them? Are there some characteristics that are more important than others? Or what if you have several potential candidates, but none of them fit all the criteria?

There are a number of basic principles to apply when making the right strategic choice of employee. The most important characteristics to consider are the employee's ability, availability, and reliability. In most circumstances, an employee with a proven ability to do a task will trump someone who has the potential to learn that task.

And remember that delegation is about optimizing your time and efforts. Availability is often more important than interest. Although an employee's interest in a task is important, it's more advantageous for you to choose someone who has the availability to complete that task in the time allotted.

And although enthusiasm for a task shows an employee's dedication, when it comes down to it, you should choose reliability over enthusiasm. An employee with proven reliability will likely get the job done to your specifications with minimal supervision.

Selecting the right person is all about balance. It's very unlikely you'll always have the perfect candidate on hand when you need to delegate tasks. But you may be able to create one.

For example, what if you have an employee who is competent at doing a task but has little time to do it, and another employee who has the time and is interested in learning the task?

In this case, you have two options. You could delegate some of the qualified employee's tasks to someone else, freeing up that person to take on your task. Alternatively, you could ask the qualified person to train the interested employee.

Question

You're about to delegate the task of updating your company web site to an employee.

Which characteristics should you prioritize when deciding an employee to select?

Options:

1. A background in web design
2. An interest in web design
3. Capacity to learn tasks quickly
4. A proven track record designing web sites
5. A passion for the work
6. An open work schedule

Answer:

Option 1: This option is correct. It's practical to choose someone who has the ability to do something, rather than someone who has to be taught.

Option 2: This option is incorrect. Interest is a key characteristic, but it's more important to prioritize the employee's ability, availability, and reliability.

Option 3: This option is incorrect. Potential is good, but a better choice would be someone who already has the ability to do the task.

Option 4: This option is correct. With a reliable employee, you'll be more likely to get the job done to your specifications with minimal supervision.

Option 5: This option is incorrect. Enthusiasm is a key characteristic, but a better choice would be someone who's available to do the task.

Option 6: This option is correct. Choosing someone who's available to do the task optimizes your time and efforts.

DELEGATION CANDIDATES

Delegation candidates

Nia is a manager at a software company. One of her tasks is to analyze the company's monthly sales data and compile a report.

Nia has determined that this is a task that could be delegated to one of her direct reports.

She has decided to talk to Albert, Hugh, and Alyssa to assess their characteristics and choose the person who would be best suited for the sales data task.

Follow along as Nia talks to Albert about the sales data task.

Nia: Albert, I wanted to talk to you about the sales data task. I need to decide this week how I'm going to delegate the responsibility.

Albert: I read the memo you sent. It sounds pretty interesting. I'm not great with numbers, but it would be good work experience for me to give this a try.

Nia: That's good to hear. Do you have the time available in your schedule to complete the report each month? We can't miss the deadline.

Albert: Yes. I can set aside a half day for it on the last Thursday of the month. I know I've missed a few deadlines in the past, but I'm working on my time management.

Nia: Have you done much work with sales data?

Albert: Not really, but I can give it a try if you need me to support you and the team.

Nia: Thanks Albert. I'll let you know what I decide to do.

Question

In his conversation with Nia, which characteristics does Albert display that could make him a candidate for delegation?

Options:

1. He has the time available in his schedule to incorporate the task
2. He has an interest in the task
3. He has the ability to do the task
4. He is reliable
5. He is enthusiastic
6. He has the potential to learn the task

Answer:

Option 1: This option is correct. Albert said that he is available to take on the task.

Option 2: This option is correct. Albert expressed interest in gaining work experience through the task.

Option 3: This option is incorrect. Albert doesn't currently have the skills he needs to do the task.

Option 4: This option is incorrect. Albert's admitted he hasn't been reliable about meeting deadlines.

Option 5: This option is correct. Albert is enthusiastic about supporting Nia and the team.

Option 6: This option is incorrect. Albert said he wasn't good with numbers. He may be able to learn the task eventually, but he doesn't show much potential.

A little later in the day, Nia meets with Hugh, one of her newer employees. Follow along as Nia talks to Hugh about delegating the task.

Nia: It's nice to be able to talk with you, Hugh. I've been meaning to compliment you on the work you did on the last project.

Hugh: Thank you. The team worked hard to meet the deadline.

Nia: I wanted to talk to you because I need to decide how I'm going to delegate the responsibility of compiling the monthly sales data.

Hugh: I'm putting together my new schedule, so if you want me to take on that task just let me know and I'll include it.

Hugh is calm

Nia: Do you think you'd have any issues with the task?

Hugh: No. I've read your memo and it seems straightforward. My first job in the industry was doing data entry, so it would be pretty routine work for me.

Nia: Thanks, Hugh. I appreciate your input. I'll be in touch. Hugh: Sure. Whatever you decide is fine with me.

Question

Which characteristics does Hugh display that could make him a candidate for delegation?

Options:
1. He is available to do the task
2. He is interested in doing the task
3. He has the ability to do the task
4. He can be relied upon to complete his work

Delegation Essentials

   5. He is enthusiastic
   6. He has the potential to learn the task

Answer:

Option 1: This option is correct. Hugh noted he could easily incorporate the task into his schedule.

Option 2: This option is incorrect. Hugh was willing to do the task, but he didn't express any particular interest.

Option 3: This option is correct. Hugh has experience with data entry.

Option 4: This option is correct. Nia congratulated Hugh on the successful completion of his last project.

Option 5: This option is incorrect. Hugh wasn't enthusiastic about taking on the task. He just indicated he would be supportive of whichever choice Nia made.

Option 6: This option is incorrect. Hugh already has the ability to do the task.

Nia's last meeting is with Alyssa. Alyssa has worked with Nia for several years. Follow along as they discuss the delegation of the data compilation task.

Nia: Thanks for dropping by, Alyssa. I wanted to get your input on the sales data compilation task I need to delegate to one of my staff members.

Alyssa: Well, I'd like to improve my skills, but I don't think I could fit it into my schedule. I know it's not going to be that time consuming, but I'm working on two projects now and they need my attention.

Alyssa is pleasant.

Nia: I trust your assessment. I've never known you to miss a deadline. Would the task itself present any other issues for you?

Alyssa: I understand the concept of what needs to be done. I'd just have to learn the software program used for the data entry and compilation. That wouldn't be difficult.

Nia: Thanks, Alyssa. I'll let you know what I decide.

Question

In her conversation with Nia, which characteristics did Alyssa display that could make her a candidate for delegation?

Options:

1. She is available to do the task
2. She is interested in doing the task
3. She has the ability to do the task
4. She is reliable
5. She is enthusiastic
6. She has the potential to learn the task

Answer:

Option 1: This option is incorrect. With her current schedule, Alyssa doesn't have the time to take on the task.

Option 2: This option is correct. Alyssa is interested in improving her skills in dealing with data.

Option 3: This option is incorrect. Alyssa doesn't know how to use the software program.

Option 4: This option is correct. Nia mentioned Alyssa has never missed a deadline.

Option 5: This option is incorrect. Alyssa wasn't particularly enthusiastic about taking on any more work.

Option 6: This option is correct. Alyssa said she could easily learn how to use the software needed for the data compilation task.

In her conversations with Albert, Hugh, and Alyssa, Nia determined that each of them has characteristics that could make them suitable for delegation. But now Nia has to decide which of her three direct reports would make the best candidate for the data compilation and reporting task.

Question

Based on their characteristics, which of Nia's direct reports would be the best candidate for delegation of the sales data compilation task?

Refer to your checklist to answer the question.

Options:

1. Albert
2. Hugh
3. Alyssa

Answer:

Option 1: This option is incorrect. Albert displayed the characteristics of interest, availability, and enthusiasm. These are good characteristics, but there is a better overall choice among Nia's direct reports.

Option 2: This is the correct option. Hugh has the characteristics of ability, availability, and reliability. Since these are the three most important characteristics, Hugh is the overall best choice for delegation.

Option 3: This option is incorrect. Alyssa showed interest, reliability, and potential. Although these are positive characteristics, there is another candidate who displays the three most important characteristics.

COMMUNICATION

Communication

Once you have selected someone to do the job, it's time to tell them about the assignment. Step three of task delegation is to assign the task to the person you've selected.

Assigning tasks to an employee consists of three steps. First you describe the task, then you motivate the person to connect to the task. Finally, you get verbal acceptance of the task.

Your first step is describing the task. Begin by explaining the greater purpose the assignment is intended to fulfill – how it will contribute to organizational goals. Employees need to know what's expected of them.

State your expectations of the employee and the standards you expect to be met. Be clear about the scope of the task and quality level you desire. If the task is complex, provide a written outline.

Make sure you communicate the details of what needs to be done, as well as criteria for completing the task. Be specific about targets that need to be hit; time lines that need to be met; and objectives that must be fulfilled.

The next step in assigning a task is to motivate the person. Motivation means gaining the employee's emotional acceptance for the task. When employees are motivated, they complete tasks because they want to, not just because they've been told to. People are motivated when they believe in what they're doing, and when they understand why the task is important to the work unit, to the organization, and to themselves.

Your employees may be motivated by responsibility, recognition, empowerment, challenge, or a combination of motivators. Knowing your employee will help you decide on the right motivational approach.

See each motivator for more information.

Responsibility

Employees motivated by responsibility need a sense of purpose to emotionally accept a task. It's important to communicate why the task is important to you and to the business goals of the organization.

Recognition

Some employees are motivated by recognition. Make sure to compliment them when you assign a task. Mention other times they've put in extra effort or performed exceptionally well.

Empowerment

Empowerment-oriented employees are motivated by being "in charge." They thrive on organizing the people and resources needed for task implementation. A good approach is to treat them more as peers than as subordinates.

Challenge

Some employees are motivated by challenge. They enjoy the opportunity to be creative and learn new things. Motivate them by asking for their opinions on how they see things being done, and listening to their ideas.

Step three of assigning a task is to get the employee's verbal acceptance of the task. This is the stage where the employee makes a commitment to completing the task.

When you seek acceptance or agreement, repeat the main points of what you've discussed to make sure you and your employee have a common understanding of the task.

Then use a closed-ended question to query your employee's acceptance. Finally, listen for the person's clear affirmative acceptance of the task.

Case Study: Question 1 of 2
Scenario

For your convenience, the case study is repeated with each question.

Pauline is an office manager. She wants to assign Raj the responsibility of ordering and tracking the inventory of the department's office supplies. Raj is an organized individual who has expressed an interest in taking on more responsibility for running the office.

Answer the task assignment questions in order.

Question

Which elements should Pauline include in her assignment of the task to Raj?

Options:

1. She should thoroughly describe the process of ordering and tracking the inventory of the department's office supplies to Raj

2. She should communicate to Raj why the task is important to the team

3. She should give Raj the task and let him set the time lines and outcomes

4. She should offer Raj a bonus to complete the task on time

Answer:

Option 1: This option is correct. The first step of task assignment is to describe the task and the outcome you expect.

Option 2: This option is correct. The second step of task assignment is to motivate the employee to emotionally accept the task. Raj seems motivated by responsibility.

Option 3: This option is incorrect. Raj should have some autonomy, but he'll need a description of the task and the outcomes Pauline expects.

Option 4: This option is incorrect. There's no indication Raj is motivated strictly by money. Pauline should motivate Raj based on what she knows about him – he's a responsible person.

Case Study: Question 2 of 2

What else should Pauline do when assigning the task to Raj?

Options:

1. She should ask Raj whether he understands and accepts the new responsibility

2. She could make sure Raj understands the consequences should he fail to complete the task

Answer:

Option 1: This is the correct option. The third step of assigning a task is to get the employee's verbal acceptance of the task.

Option 2: This option is incorrect. Anticipating failure won't engage or inspire Raj.

ASSIGNING TASKS

Assigning tasks

Your approach to assigning a task should involve clear, straightforward communication. You should impart the key information without micromanaging. Make sure to use a positive tone. Don't focus on what the employee shouldn't do, or what might go wrong. It's also valuable to employ questions to check for understanding and agreement on deliverables and deadlines.

Nia is a manager at a software company. Follow along as Nia assigns a task to her employee Elly.

Nia: Elly, I'd like you to take on the responsibility of doing our department's monthly market analysis report. Are you familiar with it?

Elly: Yes. I read it each month.

Nia: Good. The data will be sent to you on the first work day of the month. We'll need an eight-page report within two weeks, in time for the board meeting. Do you have any questions about the process?

Elly: Who's going to send the data to me? I don't want to be chasing after it each month so I won't be late with the report.

Elly is concerned.

Nia: Tim will send the data over from the IT Department. And I'm sure you won't be late, Elly. You're my most organized staff member. That's why I'm trusting you with this task.

Elly: Thanks.

Nia: At the start of each month, you'll get the data from Tim to compile an eight-page report for presentation at the next board meeting. Will you be able to do this task for me?

Elly: Yes, I will. Thanks for the opportunity.

Nia correctly followed the steps of assigning a task. First, she described the targets and time lines of the task. Next, she used a compliment to motivate Elly. Then, she gained Elly's verbal acceptance of the task.

Nia also demonstrated good communication skills. Her description of the task was clear. She used questions to check Elly's understanding and gain Elly's acceptance of the task.

She also made sure to use a positive tone, particularly when she was motivating Elly.

MONITORING PROGRESS AND GIVING FEEDBACK

Monitoring progress and giving feedback

Delegation doesn't end with assigning a task to an employee. Delegation of tasks means giving someone else the responsibility and authority to do something that you would otherwise do yourself. But as a manager, the ultimate responsibility for a delegated task still belongs to you. You may not be doing the task, but you'll still need to evaluate and measure the extent to which the task objectives are being fulfilled.

Step four of task delegation is to monitor performance. This step involves the post-assignment activities of managing the progress of the delegated task, and giving feedback on performance to the employee implementing that task.

One of the greatest challenges for managers is making sure their employees don't fail the tasks they're assigned.

After all, if your employees fail, your reputation could be damaged, and you may end up having to do the task yourself.

If your employees don't make progress, or proceed in the wrong direction, it's best to find out early. Then you give them direction or supply resources to get them back on track before the issue spirals out of control.

Monitoring progress also helps you keep your employees informed of any changes in the scope or objectives of the task.

Technological, process, or strategic changes can all affect the implementation of a task over time. In fact, you should expect that there may be changes to all but the most basic or routine tasks.

Monitoring gives you an opportunity to address any outside or higher-level influences before any serious consequences arise.

Nia is a manager at a software company. Her employee Elly's task is to produce a market analysis report for the company's monthly board meeting. Follow along as Nia monitors Elly's progress.

Nia: Elly, I'm touching base to see how you're progressing with this month's market analysis report.

Elly: Pretty well. I'll have it done in time for the board meeting on the 15th of the month.

Nia: That's why I wanted to talk to you. The board meeting has been moved up a week. We'll need the report by the 8th.

Elly: But that just gives me a week. I haven't got the data from Tim in IT yet.

Elly is worried.

Nia: I'll request that Tim get you the data right away. And Albert will be responsible to assist you. Will that allow you to complete the report on time?

Delegation Essentials

Elly: Yes. If I get the data and Albert helps out, I'll get it done. Thanks Nia.

Elly is relieved.

Nia recognized the benefits of monitoring Elly. She checked on Elly's progress and made sure to inform her of a change in the scope of the task. Then she gave Elly direction and supplied her with resources to help her stay on track, despite the change in plans.

Question

Why is it important to monitor the progress of a delegated task?

Options:

1. It can help you find out early if the task is off track
2. It improves chances of a successful conclusion
3. It gives you an opportunity to address any influences with the potential to result in serious consequences
4. Your employees will fail without your input
5. It means that if things go wrong, you won't be held responsible

Answer:

Option 1: This option is correct. It's best to discover issues early, so you can get things back on track before the process spirals out of control.

Option 2: This option is correct. Monitoring progress allows you to provide your employees with advice or assistance that keeps them focused on the right outcome.

Option 3: This option is correct. Monitoring progress gives you the opportunity to address issues that have potential serious consequences.

Option 4: This option is incorrect. Tasks are assigned because employees have the ability to handle them. Your job is to evaluate the extent to which the task objectives are being fulfilled.

Option 5: This option is incorrect. As a manager, the ultimate responsibility for a delegated task still belongs to you.

DELEGATION PRACTICES

Delegation practices

The best way to ensure successful delegation is to maintain an adequate level of control over the task. How much control you need to retain is a matter of balance. The level of control will depend on both the task and on the employee to whom you've delegated that task. The more experienced and reliable the employee, the less supervision is needed. But the more critical the task, the more cautious you should be, particularly if your reputation depends on it.

Of course, you can't be on hand to solve every problem involving a task you've delegated to an employee. Doing so would defeat the purpose of delegating the task in the first place. But some managers fall prey to two major monitoring issues – micromanaging and taking back work. Both issues stem from a desire to control decision-making, rather than encouraging initiative in their employees.

See each issue for more information.

Micromanaging

Micromanagers can't let go of telling people what to do, and how to do it. They refuse to relinquish control, and they second-guess employee decisions. Employees feel mistrusted and may lose the confidence to make competent decisions on their own.

A good manager monitors task delegation by being available without being intrusive, and by focusing on results rather than process.

Taking back work

There may be situations when you need to reassess an employee's ability to complete a task successfully. But it's important not to fall into the trap of taking back the work you've assigned at the first sign of trouble. In most cases, your employee will be able to work through the issues with a little guidance.

Question

Which statements illustrate good practices to follow when monitoring performance?

Options:

1. Focus on the employee's results, not process
2. Be available to help your employees work through issues
3. Make sure your employees know exactly how you want each task done
4. Make sure to take back the task if the employee doesn't meet your expectations

Answer:

Option 1: This option is correct. As long as your employee is meeting the standards and objectives of the assigned task, there's no reason to criticize the way things get done.

Option 2: This option is correct. Good managers help employees work through issues, rather than dictate how the work should be done.

Option 3: This option is incorrect. Micromanaging can be detrimental to the task delegation process. A good manager isn't intrusive.

Option 4: This option is incorrect. It's a much better option to work with and help the employee complete the task and learn from the experience.

GIVING FEEDBACK

Giving feedback

How do you react when someone near you is whining or complaining about how bad someone or something is? This type of behavior may get your attention, but it's unlikely it will ever get your support or respect. Now reflect on how it feels when someone communicates with you in a positive way. It's likely you'll be a lot more receptive to what that person has to say.

As a manager, you'll need to communicate all sorts of things to your employees when you're monitoring performance. In fact, feedback is an essential component of good delegation.

Feedback lets your employees know what they're doing that's having a positive effect. And it helps them change behavior that's ineffective.

There are five basic characteristics of good feedback:
- it's descriptive, not judgmental
- it's specific to the situation
- it's timely
- it's open, and

- it offers practical advice

The first characteristic of good feedback is that it's descriptive rather than judgmental. Descriptive feedback focuses on describing what you've observed, rather than criticizing the person.

For example, instead of saying, "You didn't do that survey very well," you could say, "Your response rate wasn't very high. Perhaps you would have had a better result with a different approach."

When feedback is handled well, employees shouldn't take it personally, or perceive it as disapproval or as a reprimand. Instead they should see it as a guide to help improve their abilities or behavior.

The second characteristic of good feedback is that it's specific. The more specific your feedback is, the more useful it will be to the person receiving it.

Rather than saying, "Your report isn't very clear," tell your employee exactly what you didn't understand and why you had difficulty understanding the report.

It's also important to be clear about positive feedback. Instead of just saying "You did a good job," list the things that were done well. For example, if the employee brings in new customers, or saves the company some money by improving a process, make it clear how these actions contributed to the employee's optimal performance.

The third characteristic of good feedback is that it's timely – given as soon as possible. You don't have to wait for a formal feedback session. With practice, you'll be able to integrate feedback comfortably and quickly into regular interactions with employees.

Make sure to engage them while memories are still fresh. For example, don't say, "Last month you didn't return one of my e-mails. What was the problem?"

Think about how much more effective your feedback would be if you mentioned it right away. You could say, "I sent you an e-mail this morning. Have you had a chance to read it?"

You may have noted that open communication should be a two-way conversation. The employee receiving the feedback needs an opportunity to reflect and respond to what you've said. Listening to your employees' input can help you improve as well. They'll have a good perspective on what you did, didn't do, or could do to help them. Asking the employee to share feelings about your feedback can often lead to a better understanding of the issue or behavior being discussed.

The fifth characteristic of good feedback is that it has to be practical. Your guidance should focus only on behavior that can be changed. For example, you shouldn't say, "You don't have the right personality for this task." But you could say, "A softer approach might elicit more cooperation from your colleagues."

Question

Match the examples of what you might say when monitoring and giving feedback to their corresponding categories, depending on whether they are appropriate or inappropriate. More than one example will match to each category.

Options:

A. "According to the schedule, your report is late. Are there any issues we should talk about?"

B. "I was pleased you finished the project a day early."

C. "What did you think about this morning's staff meeting?"

D. "You should always check with me before you make any decisions."

E. "You did a poor job with the brochure. I'll make corrections."

F. "It might help if you were more artistic."

Targets:
1. Appropriate
2. Inappropriate

Answer:

Good feedback is descriptive, rather than judgmental; it's also specific, timely, open, and practical.

Inappropriate monitoring includes micromanaging or taking back work from an employee. Good feedback isn't vague and doesn't involve disapproval, or criticism of the employee as a person.

OVERCOMING DELEGATION PROBLEMS

Overcoming Delegation Problems

When things go wrong in delegation, you should examine whether you've created or contributed to the problem. People make four common mistakes when delegating work. To avoid overcommitting your best people, balance workloads evenly among the whole team. Give clear direction for delegated tasks so people know your priorities. Don't expect everything to be perfect – learn to live with "good enough." And establish lines of communication between your employees and others they need to deal with in the organization.

To diagnose employee problems that affect delegated tasks, ask relevant questions. Note where your employees have insufficient support or resources or blame others for their mistakes. Understanding employee problems can help you to resolve issues and support your staff.

Some common problems that stem from skills deficiencies are the inability to make decisions, allowing simple problems to present major roadblocks, poor time management skills, or the lack of technical know-how. These problems can be resolved by providing training.

If your employees lack motivation, they might resist taking on work. You can help them by setting goals, providing support, and giving feedback. Employees who take on too much work risk burning out. You can help by making sure their workload isn't too heavy and by giving them positive feedback. Employees who lack confidence might come to you with every problem. You can help by asking their opinion, reinforcing correct answers, and letting them know you have faith in them.

Many delegation problems can be traced back to mistakes made by the delegator, employee skills deficiencies, or employee attitudes. To solve a delegation problem, ask your employees questions to find the cause of the problem. Then take the appropriate steps to resolve the issue.

EXAMINING YOURSELF

Examining yourself

Things don't always run smoothly when you delegate work. When problems arise, your first reaction may be to blame the employee you delegated the work to. But the first person you should look at is yourself. As a delegator, you can create or contribute to problems that slow things down. Were the instructions for the task clear? Did you give your employee enough guidance? Should you have delegated the task at all, or should you have completed it yourself?

You may have noted in your response that sometimes problems arise not because of employee failings, but because of a manager's poor delegation skills. Perhaps your employee doesn't understand the task details because you haven't explained them clearly. Maybe the employee doesn't know the deadline. Maybe the result is not what you expected. When this happens, examine your own behavior. Could you have changed the outcome by acting differently? Learn from your mistakes so things go better next time.

Question

Which statement represents one way that a manager's poor delegation skills can cause tasks to fail?

Options:

1. The employee hasn't been told all the requirements for the task

2. The employee would prefer to be working on something else

3. The employee is too indecisive to figure out the best way to carry out the task

Answer:

Option 1: This is the correct option. Explaining the task poorly is a common mistake made by delegators.

Option 2: This option is incorrect. Although it's important to choose the right person for the job, lack of motivation is not a problem related to delegation skills.

Option 3: This option is incorrect. Having trouble making decisions is a problem related to employee skills rather than delegator error.

SOLVING COMMON DELEGATION MISTAKES

Solving common delegation mistakes

Four common mistakes that delegators make are overcommitting top performers, giving unclear direction, nitpicking and expecting perfection, and failing to set up adequate communication with other departments.

See each common delegation mistake to learn more.

Overcommitting top performers

Even in the most talented teams, there's usually someone who outperforms the rest. It's tempting to assign as much work as possible to your best people. You know the job will be done well and to specifications, and you don't have to worry about mistakes that can hold things up.

But your top people could burn out if they're overburdened. The rest of your team could become discouraged from your lack of confidence in them. And if they're not given the opportunity to perform to the best of their ability, they have no chance to improve.

Giving unclear direction

Delegation Essentials

Many delegated tasks fail because employees haven't been given clear instructions or haven't understood their manager's intentions. You need to be sure that your employees understand exactly what's required of them. Even if you're giving them discretion in how they perform the task, you need to be clear about what output you expect and which elements of the task are most important to you.

It's easy to assume that you and your employee are both working from the same starting point, but it's not necessarily so. If you don't outline your priorities clearly, you could end up with an unexpected result.

Nitpicking and expecting perfection

You expect good results from your team when you delegate a task. But remember that everyone makes mistakes. There's a difference between asking your employees to work to the best of their ability and expecting them to do everything exactly right – or exactly as you would have done it yourself.

Criticizing every minor error can make employees frustrated. They might try to avoid accepting tasks from you because they feel like they can't satisfy you. And if you're always harsh with people who make mistakes while trying something new, you're likely to discourage innovation in your employees.

Failing to set up communication

Your employees aren't working in a vacuum. Even if you've given them the information and instructions that they need to complete the task, they'll most likely have to rely on others within the organization to get the job done.

Sometimes, employers forget that their employees might not have the same interdepartmental lines of communication that employers have. If your employees don't have structures to help them communicate with the people they need to reach, they might find it hard to get the support they need to finish their task.

The first common mistake, overcommitting your top performers, can be avoided by keeping an eye on your employees' workloads. Make sure to delegate tasks in a way that evenly distributes work among the team. Try to develop your less talented employees by giving them tasks that enable them to learn and to perform at their best – they might surprise you!

Consider this example. Ron has two direct reports, Sarah and Miguel. Sarah always gets the job done well, and Ron knows he can count on her to deliver reports to deadline without much direction. Miguel is less confident about writing, so he often needs to ask for help.

Ron needs a report for a meeting, and he knows Sarah is working on another project. But he asks her to put aside her current task and get started on the report.

By not trusting Miguel to get the job done, Ron made him feel undervalued. Sarah's worried that her original project won't be completed on time, and she's overstretched trying to juggle both tasks. If Ron had distributed his team's workload better and had more faith in Miguel, he could have achieved a better result. With a little coaching, Miguel could have written the report and learned for the future – and Ron could have avoided overcommitting Sarah.

The second mistake delegators often make is giving unclear direction. You should make sure your employees thoroughly understand what you need. If they don't, you must ascertain the missing details and provide them. For example, Bill asks Anna to draft an operating budget and to write assessments for two new employees. But he's forgotten to tell her which task is more important. So he gets assessments that could have waited, and the budget that he really needs isn't ready.

Question

Match the common delegation problems with their solutions. Each problem may have more than one solution.

Options:

A. Overcommitting top performers
B. Giving unclear direction

Targets:

1. Examine your employees' workloads and make sure to distribute work evenly

2. Let your employees know what you expect and what your priorities are

3. Ascertain missing details and provide them

4. Develop less talented employees by giving them tasks that challenge them

Answer:

Try to balance workloads so that nobody is doing more than they should be. That way, you won't overburden your best people and cause them to burn out.

When you delegate work, your employees need to understand what you want, or else you might find the results are out of tune with what you expect.

You need to make sure that you've given clear instructions. If elements of the task are unclear, give employees the knowledge they need.

By helping less talented employees to develop, you can make sure you're not overburdening top performers. And you're less likely to discourage your team.

The third mistake is expecting perfection from your employees. For example, Heidi needs someone to compile sales targets for the next month. But nobody wants to take on the job. Her employees know that whatever they do, Heidi will find fault. She can't accept that other people's ways of doing things might have merit, even if they're not what she would have done.

The solution to the problem is to realize that things can't always be perfect. You need to learn to settle for "good enough" whenever possible. Don't accept shoddy work – but don't let perfectionism lead you to dismiss good work because it isn't flawless. Try to be fair in assessing ways of doing things that don't mesh perfectly with your own. Support your team, and be open to their different perspectives.

Try to use mistakes as a way to teach the correct way to do things. That way, you won't discourage people from doing their best, and your employees won't be unwilling to take on work.

The final mistake is failing to set up adequate communication between your employees and the people they need to access to get the job done. You need to make sure everyone understands the importance of cooperating. You have to establish clear lines of communication so your employees get the support they need.

For instance, Amrit's going on vacation, so she delegates a time-sensitive task to Mark. He needs to liaise with the Human Resources Department and set up interviews for an upcoming job opening. When she gets back, she finds that the interviews haven't been arranged. Mark explains that he tried to get it done, but his colleagues in Human Resources wouldn't allow him access to the files he needed – so he had to abandon the project until Amrit returned.

Amrit is used to working with colleagues outside her department, so she didn't realize that they might not be as quick to cooperate with Mark as they are with her. She should have contacted Human Resources before she left and made sure that they understood Mark was acting on her instructions and had her support.

Question

Match the common delegation problem with the appropriate solution. Each problem may have more than one solution.

Options:

A. Nitpicking and expecting perfection
B. Failing to set up communication

Targets:

1. Learn to accept good work and try to be open to other people's perspectives
2. Make sure your employees have the support they need across the organization
3. Be fair in assessing ways of doing things that aren't exactly like yours
4. Remember that employees don't necessarily have the same communication channels as you

Answer:

Don't let the desire to make things perfect prevent you from recognizing good work – sometimes "good enough" will do.

Establish lines of communication between your employees and the people they need to work with in other departments.

Try not to let your own approach cloud your judgment of other ways of doing things.

Don't expect people to set up their own lines of communication – help employees cooperate to get the job done.

When things go wrong, sometimes there's more than one problem involved. Consider Kirsten, a team leader. When she asks for volunteers for a project, most of her team stays silent – they know Kirsten will complain if their work doesn't meet her exacting standards. Taku volunteers, even though he's working on two other projects, and Kirsten allocates the task to him. She knows he'll get the job done – but he's overstretched, and the rest of the team is disaffected.

Question

Based on Kirsten and Taku's problem, which statements represent good actions Kirsten could take to improve the situation?

Options:

1. Kirsten should try to spread the work around more evenly among the members of her team, and not overburden Taku just because he's competent and willing

2. Kirsten could relax her standards a little, and learn to support her team when they make mistakes, rather than criticizing them

3. Kirsten should ignore her team's feelings about the issue – she's in charge, and their opinions about her style of leadership don't matter

4. Kirsten should ensure her team understands what she's asking of them – they probably haven't volunteered because they aren't clear on her requirements

Answer:

Option 1: This option is correct. Kirsten is running the risk of overcommitting Taku because he's one of her best performers. She needs to delegate more to the rest of the team, or he could burn out.

Option 2: This option is correct. Kirsten wants everything to be perfect, but her team feels like they can't satisfy her, so they don't want to try. She needs to accept that sometimes mistakes will be made and try to use them as a means of teaching her employees rather than a reason to reprimand them.

Option 3: This option is incorrect. Kirsten needs to learn to communicate more effectively with her team. She should make sure that everyone involved in tasks can talk to the people they need to get the job done – and that includes herself!

Option 4: This option is incorrect. The team knows that Kirsten has high standards, and they're avoiding accepting work from her because they understand too well that she's looking for more than they think they can deliver. She needs to support them better to build confidence and let them know she has faith in them.

x

DETERMINING THE PROBLEM

Determining the problem

Sometimes, when things go wrong with delegation, employee problems are to blame. There are two kinds of problems that can affect your employees' ability to get the job done: skills deficiencies and attitudes toward work.

To help you uncover and identify problems related to skills deficiencies, you need to talk to your employees. Ask questions to find out about the task's progress. Listen for points of frustration. Note where your employees feel they have insufficient support or resources. They might think they need more authority, more assistance, or more money to get the job done. If the complaint seems valid, take steps to get the employees what they need.

Sometimes, your employee's attitude is at fault. So you should also note when the employee blames the circumstances or colleagues for the failure. People often blame other people for poor performance before taking responsibility for mistakes.

Conduct your own investigation to find out whether your employee's claims are justified. You may find that your employee is right, and the task is failing for reasons beyond your employee's control. If so, you need to provide support by addressing the problem or talking to the people involved.

But you may find that your employee is simply shifting the blame. In that case, you may be facing an attitude-related issue that will need to be dealt with.

Question

Which statements represent issues you should try to uncover when questioning employees about delegation problems?

Options:

1. Your employee has insufficient resources to get the job done

2. Your employee is unfairly blaming other people for mistakes

3. Your employee is having problems getting other people to cooperate with them

4. Your employee has opinions on who you should delegate particular tasks to

5. Your employee is not loyal to you and to the team

Answer:

Option 1: This option is correct. If your employee says resources are insufficient, you should check whether it's true. Then you should provide the tools needed to finish the job.

Option 2: This option is correct. Sometimes, people blame others rather than accepting responsibility for their own failings. If you find your employee has this kind of performance issue, you can take steps to deal with it.

Option 3: This option is correct. When your employees complain of lack of support, you need to investigate whether that's correct. If it is, address the problem.

Option 4: This option is incorrect. Your employee might well have good suggestions for who should be assigned what task. But it won't help solve the problem with the task you've assigned.

Option 5: This option is incorrect. How loyal your employees are might affect their work in general. But you need to look for problems more directly related to delegation, such as whether they have sufficient resources and whether they're shifting blame.

Asking the right questions can help you to identify the issues holding back delegated tasks – and it's a good first step in addressing your employees' problems. It shows your team members that you're interested in their point of view. It lets them understand that you're willing to make changes to support them. This can help them to be more receptive to the idea of making changes themselves.

It's important to be able to diagnose problems that affect your employees' abilities to carry out delegated tasks. If you understand all the issues at play, you can take steps to solve the problem. And knowing their particular problems can enable you to figure out the best way to help your employees develop. Some employees might need more experience, some might need help increasing their skills, and some might simply need more confidence.

Consider Tonya, whose direct report, Mario, is having trouble completing a task she's assigned. She questions him, and he complains that he can't get the help he needs to finish his task.

Tonya conducts her own investigation, and she learns that Mario hasn't asked anyone to help him. She knows that Mario may have a performance issue, since he's blamed other people for his own mistake.

Now that she understands Mario's problem a little better, she talks to him to find out more. She discovers that Mario doesn't like asking other people for support because he lacks confidence in his own abilities. She's able to help him understand that collaborating with others isn't a sign of incompetence. And he works better in future as a result.

Question

Which statements represent the benefits of being able to correctly diagnose employee problems with delegated tasks?

Options:

1. If you understand all the issues at play, you might know what to do to resolve the situation

2. Understanding your employees' problems can help you to find the best way of helping them to develop

3. You can avoid delegating work to more difficult employees

4. You can allow employees with problems to choose tasks that don't challenge them

Answer:

Option 1: This option is correct. It's easier to find the appropriate solution to a problem if you understand all the issues involved.

Option 2: This option is correct. All your employees have their own needs, and finding out their specific problems can help you figure out how to build their skills.

Option 3: This option is incorrect. You need to use your team effectively by delegating work evenly among them. But you can help your employees address their specific problems to become better able to carry out the tasks you delegate.

Option 4: This option is incorrect. It's better in the long term for your employees to overcome their problems, where possible. Once you know their limitations, you can help them to expand their skill sets by providing training.

IMPROVING EMPLOYEE SKILLS

Improving employee skills

Sometimes, an employee's lack of skills is behind problems with delegated tasks. There are some signs that you should watch for to find out if your employee has inadequate skills. Your employee might be unable to complete the task you've assigned, the task might be completed poorly, or the employee may have to ask for help too frequently. When you discover your employee has a skills deficiency, you should try to provide training to help improve skills.

Skills deficiencies can lead to some common issues. Your employees might be unable to make decisions that allow them to proceed with the project. You might find that simple problems seem to present massive roadblocks to the task's progress. Your employees might have poor time management skills that cause things to be delayed. Or your employees might have insufficient technical know-how to get the job done.

The first issue is being unable to make decisions. To solve this, you should provide training in decision- making processes. As your employee learns to make decisions, offer support by assigning different

levels of responsibility. Ask indecisive employees to identify problems and suggest solutions for approval. Ask more confident employees to choose a solution and check with you before acting on it. As your employees become more assured, you can ask them to resolve issues themselves and keep you informed of their actions.

Consider Luke, whose direct report, Dominique, is late with a presentation he asked her to write. Luke talks to Dominique about her issue, and she tells him that she can't figure out how to present the information. The dilemma has perplexed her so much that she hasn't started writing yet.

Luke provides Dominique with training on the best way to make decisions. Then he asks her to identify the best solution to her problem and to come back to him with her decision. Dominique identifies two solutions: she could present the information chronologically, or she could use a thematic approach.

Dominique submits these suggestions to Luke so he can approve one of them. After examining the alternatives, Luke tells Dominique the information should probably be presented chronologically. Dominique agrees and, now that the decision is made, she is able to finish the task.

Question

A manager has three direct reports: Rudy, Felicity, and Deborah. Rudy is not good at making decisions, Felicity is a little more assured, and Deborah is the most confident. Match each employee with the appropriate delegation strategy.

Options:

A. Rudy
B. Felicity
C. Deborah

Targets:

1. Come up with solutions and present them for approval
2. Identify the best solution and check with the manager before implementing it
3. Deal with the issue and keep the manager informed

Answer:

Rudy should be supported in learning how to make decisions by asking him to think of solutions by himself and then present them to his manager for a final decision.

Felicity is growing more confident in making decisions, so she should be asked to come up with a good solution and bring it to her manager for sign-off.

Since Deborah's relatively comfortable making decisions, her manager can trust her to solve the problem, as long as she provides information on what she's doing.

For some employees, simple problems turn into massive roadblocks – the second common skills issue. These employees should be taught a good problem-solving strategy. One useful strategy consists of seven steps:

- define the problem as it appears to you
- assemble the facts, different stakeholders' opinions, and any relevant impressions
- redefine the problem, in light of the new information you've gathered
- come up with possible solutions
- examine the different solutions and choose the best option
- carry out the decision you've made, and

- examine the results of your decision

Consider, for example, Glen, whose employee, Olga, has hit a snag in completing her delegated task. She was asked to schedule a meeting with various members of the department, but she can't find a time that suits everyone. She's unable to find a way out of this simple problem.

Glen teaches Olga a problem-solving technique. Together, they define the problem: people's schedules are different, so there's no time that suits everyone. They talk to each person who's supposed to attend the meeting and find out their different scheduling conflicts. Once they know the facts, they're able to redefine the problem. There is a time that suits most people, but one team member has a conference call scheduled for that time.

They think of some solutions: find another time, conduct the meeting without the team member, or arrange to reschedule the department member's call. They decide the best thing to do is to reschedule the call, and Glen arranges it. The meeting can be held, and Olga has learned how to approach similar problems in the future.

The third common issue is poor time management. If you find that your employees are having trouble getting things done on time, first check their workloads. Examine how they're using their time. This can help you to ascertain whether you've allocated them too much work.

You might find that your employees' time problems are coming from inefficiency. If so, you need to provide training to help them develop better time management skills. Tips to improve time management might include prioritizing tasks, breaking large tasks into smaller tasks, or limiting distractions.

For example, Linda's employee, Bhadrak, was asked to check the store's inventory and contact suppliers to restock items. But he has only managed to call two of ten suppliers. Linda examines his workload and finds he should have had time to get the calls made. He has been distracted by less important tasks. She solves the problem by offering Bhadrak time management training. Once he's learned to prioritize better, he succeeds in completing the delegated task.

The fourth skills deficiency issue is related to insufficient technical know-how. Different tasks require different skill sets. Your employees might need to know how to use certain software. They might need to understand what conduct is appropriate at a business meeting. Or they might have to know how to conduct performance checks on a supplier. If your employees don't have the skills they need to complete the task you've delegated, find a way to train them in the skills they need.

Question

Sally has asked her employee, Travis, to input suppliers' invoices into the company's billing system, but he hasn't completed the task. Sally speaks to Travis, and he tells her his computer doesn't have the software needed to do the job. He didn't understand how to install it, so he started work on an assignment that's due next month instead.

What should Sally do to resolve the situation?

Options:

1. Sally should offer Travis training in managing his time better

2. Sally should show Travis how to install the software he needs

3. Sally should ask Travis to identify a solution and present it for her approval

4. Sally should teach Travis to define the problem better

Answer:

Option 1: This option is correct. Travis needs to learn how to prioritize more important tasks, so he could benefit from acquiring better time management skills.

Option 2: This option is correct. Sally should provide Travis with the resources and technical knowledge he needs to get the job done.

Option 3: This option is incorrect. Identifying a solution for approval would be a good way to help him learn decision making, but Travis's problem is related to a lack of technical knowledge and poor prioritization of tasks.

Option 4: This option is incorrect. Travis understands the issue, so he doesn't need training in defining the problem. He needs extra resources and better time management skills.

LACKING IN MOTIVATION

Lacking in motivation

Sometimes, employees' attitudes toward delegation can lead to problems. A sign that you're facing a problem stemming from employees' attitudes is that your employee doesn't consult you about the task and won't talk about the task's progress. Another sign is that your employee wants to consult you about every detail and won't accept responsibility for the task.

There are some common problems that come from employee attitudes to delegation. Your employee might be lacking in motivation. You might find an employee is taking on too much work. Or your employee might be lacking in confidence.

The first problem related to employee attitudes is lack of motivation. Some employees resist or resent delegated tasks because they don't want to do any additional work. When their manager tries to give them something to do, they might make excuses. They might complain of being overstretched or ask why someone else can't do it.

The performance equation says that performance is equal to ability multiplied by motivation. Employees' ability can be enhanced by training. But their motivation is down to their commitment and desire to get the job done. Your employees need to have both ability and motivation if they're to perform well.

If you allow your unmotivated employees to avoid tasks, you risk overburdening other team members. And letting them shift tasks to others isn't helping your unmotivated employees to develop.

You may have noted in your answer that when you encounter resistance due to lack of motivation, you need to be firm with your employees. Don't allow them to refuse to act. Be open and honest with your employees, but use your authority to make sure they complete the task.

There are three steps you can use to help improve employee motivation:

- First, set performance goals. Employees should have a clear understanding of what's expected of them.
- Next, provide performance assistance. Check your employees' tasks regularly, provide milestones for them to meet, and offer training and support where needed.
- Finally, make sure you give feedback on their performance. Both positive and negative feedback can help reinforce what your employees have learned and encourage better performance in future.

Consider Chen, who has asked her employee, Ramon, to compile some figures. He's refused to complete the task.

Delegation Essentials

Ramon has a history of resisting delegated tasks, so Chen decides it's time to speak to him. Follow along as they discuss the situation.

Chen: Ramon, I know that you feel you're overburdened, but you have to understand that when I ask you to take on a task, it's because I need you to do it. I've examined your workload, and you have the time to compile these figures, so I'm going to assign this task to you.

Chen is concerned.

Ramon: I know it seems like I have the time, but actually, I'm very busy. Can't you ask someone else to do it?

Ramon is disgruntled.

Chen: No, Ramon – this is your task. We'll do it like this – let's set some goals for the job. This week, you can find the source material for the figures, and then come back to me and we'll go through the material. Then you can start putting them together. Does that sound reasonable?

Chen is firm.

Ramon: Yes, but what if I can't find the figures? I'm going to need other departments to get them to me – they'll probably hold things up.

Ramon is hesitant.

Chen: Don't worry, Ramon, I'll make sure that you have the support you need. I'll speak to the other departments and make sure they're ready to work with you. And when you've got everything done, we'll talk about how it went, and I can give you some feedback to help you for the future. Are you clear on everything now?

Chen is supportive.

Ramon: Yes, I suppose so. I'll get started on it today.
Ramon agrees, reluctantly.

Ramon was resistant to taking on the job. But Chen was firm with him and didn't let him pass it on to someone else. She set goals and reassured him that he'd have the support he needed. And when he's finished, she'll give him feedback to help him improve.

In time, this strategy should help make Ramon a more motivated and less resistant employee.

Question

Which option represents a good way to deal with an employee who resists delegated tasks?

Options:

1. Speak to the employee and set performance goals
2. Allow the employee to choose which tasks to complete
3. Delegate tasks to another employee
4. Immediately transfer the employee to another department

Answer:

Option 1: This is the correct option. You can improve employee motivation by setting performance goals, providing support, and giving regular feedback.

Option 2: This option is incorrect. Letting your employee dictate what they will and won't do is likely to alienate other employees, as well as causing inconvenience for you.

Option 3: This option is incorrect. You risk overburdening other employees if you ask them to take on extra work to make up for your unmotivated employee.

Option 4: This option is incorrect. Before taking drastic action, you could try discussing the situation with your employee, and taking steps to help improve motivation.

TAKING ON TOO MUCH WORK

Taking on too much work

The second problem related to employee attitudes is taking on too much work. Some employees have trouble saying no. Maybe your employees enjoy challenges, or they thrive on the praise they get for finishing tasks. Maybe they hope to be noticed by their manager to get a promotion. Or maybe they don't want to let anyone down, so they overcommit themselves rather than displease someone.

It's tempting to allow this kind of employee to get on with things. You know you have a willing volunteer for the job, so that's one less thing you have to worry about. But by allowing your employees to overcommit themselves, you risk letting them burn out. People can't work beyond their capacity all the time. Eventually, they'll start to miss deadlines, make mistakes, and leave work undone.

Don't assign your willing employees too much work. If they're having trouble keeping up, help them rebalance their workload by reassigning tasks to other employees.

Delegation Essentials

Give them plenty of positive feedback, so they feel like they're valued and don't need to prove themselves. Employees who are eager to work are valuable. Don't allow them to become disaffected by overworking themselves!

For example, Celeste volunteers for every task in the office. From organizing files to drafting budgets, Celeste will gladly take anything on. But she's started making mistakes. Her employer, Pierre, talks to her. He tells her that everyone appreciates her efforts and that she's a hugely valuable team member. Then he reassigns some of the work she's taken on, so she has some time to catch her breath. And he makes sure she takes less work on in future.

Question

Imagine you have two talented employees, Janet and Noah. Janet resists taking on work. And Noah is always happy to take on tasks, even when his workload is too heavy.

What should you do to help them perform at their best?

Options:

1. Rebalance both employees' workloads, and help Janet by providing goals, support, and feedback

2. Allow Noah to take on whatever he likes, and make Janet keep up with him by assigning her more work

3. Give Noah positive feedback in Janet's hearing to motivate her by letting her know she's less valued

Answer:

Option 1: This is the correct option. You should make sure Noah hasn't taken on too much, and increase Janet's motivation by giving her goals, support, and feedback.

Option 2: This option is incorrect. Letting Noah take on as much work as he wants could cause him to burn out. You need to make sure his workload is manageable.

Option 3: This option is incorrect. Giving Noah positive feedback is a good idea, so he doesn't think he has to prove himself. But Janet won't become more motivated by feeling that she's not valued.

It's important to be able to recognize the problems behind different employee behaviors. That way, you'll know the best thing to do to get the task back on track.

Consider the example of Bernadette, who has asked her employee, Felix, to take charge of some redecorating work that's being done in the office. When she checks up on the task's progress, she finds it hasn't been started.

She speaks to Felix, and it seems he's forgotten that he agreed to take responsibility for the job. He's trying to get through a large volume of work that he'd already taken on. He assures her that he's doing the best he can, and he feels terrible about slipping up.

Question

Based on what you've learned, what should Bernadette say to Felix to help resolve the situation?

Options:

1. "Let's reassign some of your tasks. I really value your work, but be careful you don't exhaust yourself." 2. "You need to get it done, Felix. I'll set some goals and give you some feedback when you're done."

3. "You're doing good work, but you need to learn to be less forgetful and take more responsibility, Felix."

4. "I'm sure you can solve the problem, Felix. I have faith in your abilities."

Answer:

Delegation Essentials

Option 1: This is the correct option. Felix has taken on too much work, and Bernadette's right to try to rebalance his workload. Her positive feedback might help him stop trying to prove himself.

Option 2: This option is incorrect. Felix's problem doesn't come from lack of motivation, so he doesn't need help setting goals. He's trying to get too many things done at once.

Option 3: This option is incorrect. Forgetting about the task probably doesn't mean Felix can't take on responsibility. It's more likely a sign he needs his workload scaled back before he burns out.

Option 4: This option is incorrect. It's good to give Felix positive feedback, but he probably needs more help rebalancing his workload so he can cope with all his tasks.

LACKING CONFIDENCE

Lacking confidence

The third problem is that some employees have the skills to get the job done, but they lack the confidence to complete the task. Maybe these employees are afraid of failure, or maybe they don't like responsibility. One indication you're facing a problem of confidence is when employees ask your help about problems you know they could solve themselves. Or maybe your employees can handle simple tasks but seem unsure how to proceed when the task is more complex.

When employees with low confidence come to you for help with a problem you think they can solve, ask them for their own opinion on what should be done. Reinforce their correct answers with positive feedback. If you think they're looking for help too often, stress that they should sometimes try to work things out by themselves. Tell them often that you have faith in them. Encourage them to take risks. And point out that making mistakes can help them learn.

Delegation Essentials

Consider Raj, whose employee, Donna, is very talented. But every time she's assigned a task, she comes to Raj with questions about every detail. She's been asked to mock up a design for a client's web site. Follow along as they discuss her latest query about the project.

Donna: I'm not sure what to do, Raj – I have two different color schemes here, and I don't know which is better. What do you think?

Donna is confused.

Raj: Thanks, Donna – they both look good to me. Which do you think the client would prefer?

Raj is supportive.

Donna: Well, I suppose since their brand image is young and vibrant, maybe the web site should have colors that get that across. So maybe this yellow scheme would work best. I don't know – maybe I'm wrong.

Donna is unsure.

Raj: That sounds absolutely right to me, Donna – good thinking! You know I wouldn't have asked you to do this task if I didn't think you were up for the job. You're one of my best designers.

Raj is supportive.

Donna: Thanks for saying that, Raj – that's good to hear. I worry that I'm not getting things right often enough. I did have an idea for an animation we could use on the site, but it's probably too much work, and it might not work in the end anyway.

Donna is pleased.

Raj: I think that sounds like a great idea, Donna – you should definitely try it out. Remember, the worst that can happen is it goes wrong – mistakes aren't the end of the world. If it doesn't work out, it'll put us on track to finding an idea that will. Good work!

Raj is supportive.

Donna: Thanks, Raj! I'll go get started on that animation!

Donna is happy.

Donna is more talented than she realizes. She already knew the answer to the question she asked. And when she received positive feedback, it turned out she had another good idea for the project. All she needed was her employer's support and belief.

With Raj's help, she'll soon have the confidence she needs to perform at the top of her ability. And she won't feel she has to look for permission to implement her ideas.

Question

Three employees have different issues with completing delegated tasks.

Match the employee with the problem that's most likely behind the performance issue.

Options:

A. Anita avoids volunteering for work – when her employer tries to assign her a task, she asks if someone else can do it

B. Lucas is overcommitted, but he still offers to do anything that needs doing

C. Ryan comes to his employer with every tiny problem that arises with his task

Targets:

1. Lacking in motivation
2. Taking on too much work
3. Lacking confidence

Answer:

Delegation Essentials

Anita resists taking on extra work, which is probably the result of a lack of motivation. Her employer needs to help her by setting goals, providing support, and giving her feedback.

Lucas takes on more work than he should, maybe out of a desire to please. His employer should make sure he isn't overburdened and give him plenty of positive feedback.

Ryan seems to lack the confidence to make decisions for himself. His employer should help him by letting him know he's trusted and encouraging him to take risks.

GLOSSARY

Glossary

A

aptitude - The ability to perform a skill well. Usually refers to a mental or intellectual ability, not a physical one.

authority - The power or right to give orders and instructions and to make decisions.

B

bias - A personal opinion, preference, or inclination toward something formed without objective justification.

blaming - Making statements that attribute fault or accountability for a negative outcome to some other person or situation.

C

closed-ended question - A question phrased to elicit a short dichotomous response.

cohesion - The degree to which members of a group work together to achieve common goals.

collaboration - 1. Work conducted jointly with others. 2. The sharing of expertise, information, and responsibility to achieve a common goal.

company - An organization that is a legal entity operating for profit. See organization.

competency - The capacity to apply and use a combination of skill, knowledge, ability, and behavior to achieve an objective.

complaint - An expression of feelings of pain, dissatisfaction, or resentment, often directed toward a specific person, object, or situation.

context - The social circumstances or environments that determine, refine, or change the implicit meaning of a communicated message.

coworker - A person working with another worker, usually at or near a similar level of authority or responsibility in the workplace hierarchy.

critical task - A task that carries an element of risk or importance and that must be performed correctly to avoid loss, damage, or delay.

D

delegation - A management approach in which the leader assigns decision-making authority to others.

dynamics - The interplay of different forces on any particular activity.

E

empathy - The ability to understand the emotional state of another.

empowerment - Giving a person the authority to make decisions without requiring specific approval. See authority.

engagement - Emotional and psychological commitment to completing tasks and attaining organizational goals and objectives.

environment - The political, strategic, or operational context within, or external to, an organization.

expert - A person who possesses specialized knowledge, skills, and competencies in a specific field or endeavor.

F

false assumption - A conclusion that is not based in fact, or is based on incomplete knowledge of the facts.

faux pas - An unintentional violation of accepted social norms, such as customs or etiquette.

feedback - Information communicated to an individual, work unit, or team about job-related performance or behavior.

G

goals - Quantifiable aims used to measure progress toward an end result.

I

influence - The power to change an outcome by affecting or controlling a course of events.

initiative - An organizational program, project, or effort that has a specific purpose, goal, and objective. See project.

M

motivation - Encouragement through incentive.

mutual agreement - An obvious or implied agreement between the employee and the company.

N

need - Something that is necessary to achieve an objective.

nonverbal communication - Unspoken or unvoiced elements of communication used to send messages, modify meaning, and convey emotion.

O

objective - A specific measurable or observable goal to be achieved over a specified period of time.

open-ended question - A question phrased to elicit an unstructured response.

organization - A defined group of people who have common goals and who follow an agreed-upon set of operating procedures to produce products and services.

outcome - The consequence of an activity.

P

performance - Actions or behaviors that support the organization's goals and that are measured in terms of an individual's proficiency.

personal behavior - Behaviors particular to an individual.

personal bias - See bias.

persuasion - A form of communication that uses logical arguments and evidence to gain support.

plan - A detailed formulation of a program of action for achieving a goal or objective.

positive reinforcement - Specific praise or rewards targeted at a subject with the purpose of increasing the future frequency of a desired behavior.

progress - Movement toward stated objectives.

project - A collaborative enterprise with a defined beginning and end that is planned to achieve specific goals and objectives.

Q

quality - Conformance to stated requirements.

R

rapport - Harmonious accord between two people, or one person and a group or audience.

resistance - Noncompliant behavior.

S

skill - The ability to perform a specific task or achieve a specific goal or objective.

status - A person's social or cultural value or standing relative to that of others.

T

tactics - Planned, directed, and controlled actions used to achieve a task.

task - A specific and individual unit of work.

time line - A linear chronological representation of a task, project, or initiative that includes dates, events, milestones, and planned outcomes.

U

undermine - To intentionally create obstacles to another individual's pursuit of success.

V

values - The common beliefs driving how tasks get accomplished within the structure of an organization.

vision - A high-level statement of the purpose and aspirations of the organization, clarifying the direction for change.

REFERENCES

References
  The Busy Manager's Guide To Delegation - 2009, Richard A. Luecke and Perry McIntosh, AMACOM
  If You Want It Done Right, You Don't Have to Do It Yourself!: The Power of Effective Delegation - 2004, Donna M. Genett, Linden Publishing
  Delegating Work - 2008, Compilation, Harvard Business School Press
  Delegating for Results, Revised Edition - 1998, Robert B. Maddux, Crisp Learning

www.ingramcontent.com/pod-product-compliance
Lightning Source LLC
Chambersburg PA
CBHW020919180526
45163CB00007B/2797